Bookvan

Testament
A Beginner's Guide

ONEWORLD BEGINNER'S GUIDES combine an original, inventive, and engaging approach with expert analysis on subjects ranging from art and history to religion and politics, and everything in between. Innovative and affordable, books in the series are perfect for anyone curious about the way the world works and the big ideas of our time.

aesthetics
africa
american politics
anarchism
animal behaviour
anthropology
anti-capitalism
aquinas
art
artificial intelligence
the bahai faith
the beat generation
the bible
biodiversity
bioterror & biowarfare
the brain
british politics
the Buddha
cancer
censorship
christianity
civil liberties
classical music
climate change
cloning
cold war
conservation
crimes against humanity
criminal psychology
critical thinking
daoism
democracy
descartes
dewey

dyslexia
energy
the enlightenment
engineering
epistemology
european union
evolution
evolutionary psychology
existentialism
fair trade
feminism
forensic science
french literature
french revolution
genetics
global terrorism
hinduism
history of science
homer
humanism
huxley
international relations
iran
islamic philosophy
islamic veil
journalism
judaism
lacan
life in the universe
literary theory
machiavelli
mafia & organized crime
magic
marx

medieval philosophy
middle east
modern slavery
NATO
nietzsche
the northern ireland conflict
nutrition
oil
opera
the palestine–israeli conflict
particle physics
paul
philosophy
philosophy of mind
philosophy of religion
philosophy of science
planet earth
postmodernism
psychology
quantum physics
the qur'an
racism
reductionism
religion
renaissance art
the roman empire
the russian revolution
shakespeare
the small arms trade
sufism
the torah
united nations
volcanoes

The New Testament

A Beginner's Guide

W. R. Telford

ONEWORLD

A Oneworld Book

This paperback edition published in 2014

Originally published in 2002 as *The New Testament: A Short Introduction: A Guide to Early Christianity and the Synoptic Gospels*

Copyright © W. R. Telford 2002, 2014

ISBN 978-1-78074-338-7
eISBN 978-1-78074-339-4 (eBook)

Typeset by Cenveo Publishing Services, Bangalore, India
Printed and bound in Denmark by Nørhaven A/S

Oneworld Publications
10 Bloomsbury Street
London WC1B 3SR
United Kingdom

To Andrena

Contents

List of tables and figures

Tables

Figures

Acknowledgements

This book was written over a period of six weeks spent at St Deiniol's Library, Hawarden in North Wales. My thanks must go, first of all, to the Trustees, Warden and Staff of the Library for all the support, help and encouragement they have offered me, not only during this period, but at all the other times when I have had the privilege and joy of working here. Particular thanks go to the Trustees for awarding me a Revd Dr Murray McGregor Memorial Scholarship, and to the Warden and Chief Librarian, the Revd Peter Francis, for his enduring friendship and assistance. For making it possible for me to have a period of study leave, my appreciation goes to my colleagues in the Department of Religious Studies at Newcastle University, and to the Dean of the Faculty of Arts, Dr Eric Cross. This book is based on a series of lectures given over the years to my first year undergraduates at Newcastle. My thanks, therefore, go to them, for the interest they have shown in the New Testament, and for the stimulation they have provided to put these lectures into published form. My gratitude also extends to Oneworld, for making it possible for me to publish *The New Testament: A Beginner's Guide*, and to its enterprising publisher, Novin Doostdar, for his patience, encouragement and good humour. Last, but certainly not least, I would like to thank, as always, my dear wife, Andrena, for being my number one supporter, for giving me the benefit of her advice and judgement, and, above all, for being, at all times, her loving, charming and cheerful self.

Preface

No other collection of writings is perhaps better served with Guides and Introductions, both scholarly and popular, than the New Testament. To supply yet another might seem at best unnecessary, at worst impertinent. Further, to offer a beginner's guide not only to the New Testament, but to early Christianity and the Synoptic Gospels as well, when others have written, at length and in depth, on these weighty subjects, and on these significant texts, might appear no less than foolhardy. Clearly, therefore, a strategy is required. This *Beginner's Guide* proceeds from the presupposition that the historical value of the New Testament writings lies in the fact that they represent (though not exclusively, as we shall see), the foundation documents of early Christianity. To understand them, one must therefore have a broad, historical awareness of the wider social, economic, political, cultural and religious context in which they were produced. To appreciate them, one must also have a more specific knowledge and understanding of the needs, circumstances and ideology of the first- and second-century Christian communities out of which they arose. To interpret them in their original context, furthermore, one must have some grasp of the methods of historical criticism which contemporary scholars apply to them (especially to the Gospels), and there is no better way to do this than to become familiar with at least some of the texts in some depth.

These presuppositions help define the strategy I have adopted in this book. Given its nature and scope, and the fact that it would be impossible to do justice to all twenty-seven of the writings which make up the New Testament, we shall proceed, therefore, in a series of ever-narrowing circles, moving from the general to the particular. In the first chapter, entitled 'The World of the New Testament', I shall be providing a survey of the creative milieu in which Christianity was born, giving due weight to the fact that this new religious movement was a product of two 'chromosomes', if you like, one provided by Hellenism, the other by the mother-religion, Judaism. The womb in which this new age child was conceived was the Roman Empire. In the second chapter, we shall examine the early church, outlining its origins and history, and commenting on the nature and development of belief and practice in the New Testament period (30–150 CE). Then, in our third and central chapter, we shall move on to the literature produced by the early church, the New Testament writings themselves. Here, I shall be pointing out the factors that led to the emergence of these writings, and offering a brief introduction to them. For more detailed information, the reader will be referred to the more specialized help that is available. In the fourth and fifth chapters, our focus will become narrower still. Here, I shall be concentrating on the special Gospel literature in which many of the traditions about Christianity's founder, Jesus, are found (in particular the Synoptic Gospels), and we shall conduct this study armed with the tools that scholars use to interpret them.

Abbreviations

Old Testament (or Hebrew Bible)

Gen.	Genesis	Ezra	Ezra	Dan.	Daniel
Exod.	Exodus	Neh.	Nehemiah	Hos.	Hosea
Lev.	Leviticus	Est.	Esther	Joel	Joel
Num.	Numbers	Job	Job	Amos	Amos
Deut.	Deuteronomy	Ps. (Pss.)	Psalm(s)	Obad.	Obadiah
Josh.	Joshua	Prov.	Proverbs	Jon.	Jonah
Judg.	Judges	Eccl.	Ecclesiastes	Mic.	Micah
Ruth	Ruth	Cant.	Canticles	Nah.	Nahum
1 Sam.	1 Samuel		(Song of Songs)	Hab.	Habakkuk
2 Sam.	2 Samuel		(Song of Solomon)	Zeph.	Zephaniah
1 Kgs	1 Kings	Isa.	Isaiah	Hag.	Haggai
2 Kgs	2 Kings	Jer.	Jeremiah	Zech.	Zechariah
1 Chron.	1 Chronicles	Lam.	Lamentations	Mal.	Malachi
2 Chron.	2 Chronicles	Ezek.	Ezekiel		

New Testament

Mt.	Matthew	Eph.	Ephesians	Heb.	Hebrews
Mk	Mark	Phil.	Philippians	Jas	James
Lk.	Luke	Col.	Colossians	1 Pet.	1 Peter
Jn	John	1 Thess.	1 Thessalonians	2 Pet.	2 Peter
Acts	Acts	2 Thess.	2 Thessalonians	1 Jn	1 John
Rom.	Romans	1 Tim.	1 Timothy	2 Jn	2 John
1 Cor.	1 Corinthians	2 Tim.	2 Timothy	3 Jn	3 John
2 Cor.	2 Corinthians	Titus	Titus	Jude	Jude
Gal.	Galatians	Phlm.	Philemon	Rev.	Revelation

[Biblical quotations are taken from the Revised Standard Version.]

Other abbreviations

Adv. Haer.	Irenaeus, *Adversus Haereses* (*Against the Heresies*)
Agric.	Tacitus, *Agricola*
Ant.	Josephus, *Antiquitates Judaicae* (*Antiquities of the Jews*)
BCE	Before the Common Era (i.e. the era common to Christianity and Judaism)
BJ	Josephus, *De Bello Judaico* (*Jewish War*)
CE	(In or of) the Common Era
2DH	Two-Document Hypothesis
Eccl. Hist.	Eusebius, *Ecclesiastical History*
ET	English Translation
IQS	*Community Rule*
LXX	Septuagint (Greek translation of the Hebrew Bible)
par.	Parallels or parallel passages (esp. in the other Synoptic Gospels)

1

The world of the New Testament

The Roman Empire

Our study begins with the world of the New Testament, and so let me offer some preliminary definitions. What do I mean by 'the world of the New Testament'? The world of the New Testament is the world of a) the Roman Empire; b) Greek language and civilization, or 'Hellenism'; and c) Jewish religion and culture. What do I mean by 'Hellenism'? The term 'Hellenism' comes from the Greek word *hellenismos* which means 'imitation of the Greeks'. Hellenism, in the words of Norman Perrin, refers to 'the culture that developed in the world conquered by Alexander the Great [in the first part of the fourth century BCE] as that world adopted the Greek language and imitated Greek ways'.[1] The Hellenistic period may be said to have extended, then, from *c.*323 BCE [i.e. after the death of Alexander] to the end (for our purposes) of the New Testament period (*c.*150 CE). As one of its two parents, Hellenism was the surrounding and nurturing ethos for early Christianity and the New Testament writings.

With these preliminary definitions in mind, let us look in turn at each of the three political and cultural backgrounds which make up 'the world of the New Testament', beginning with the Roman Empire. At the height of its power, the Roman Empire encompassed an area that stretched from Britain southwards as far as Morocco, then eastwards as far as Arabia, then north to Turkey and Romania and finally westwards along the Danube to the Rhine. From its legendary founding by Romulus and Remus in 753 BCE, the little city-state of Rome had slowly risen to occupy this dominating influence in the Mediterranean world, particularly after North Africa was brought into its orbit with the defeat of the Carthaginians. By a series of military victories or astute alliances, Greece, Sicily, Sardinia, Corsica, Crete, Cyprus and Asia Minor were gradually brought under its sway. Syria and its neighbouring principality, Judaea, fell to Pompey in 64/63 BCE, Europe fell to Caesar in the Gallic Wars, Egypt to Octavian after the defeat of Antony and Cleopatra at the battle of Actium (31 BCE), and Britain (at least its 'softer' parts) to Claudius in 43 CE.

In the days of the Republic, power lay in the hands of an oligarchy ('rule by the few'), a situation threatened by the imperial pretensions of Julius Caesar. These pretensions were 'nipped in the bud' with his assassination in 44 BCE at the hands of the republican conspirators, Brutus, Cassius *et al.* Brutus and Cassius were in turn defeated by Antony and Octavian who divided the Empire between them, Octavian ruling the western part (with its capital at Rome) and Antony and Queen Cleopatra the eastern part (with its capital at Alexandria). With the defeat of Antony and Cleopatra at the battle of Actium, and their consequent suicide, mastery of the whole Roman world passed to Octavian.

By 27 BCE, Octavian had subdued the Empire, and had established peace. He had handed the Empire back to the Senate and people of Rome, and was in turn pronounced *princeps*, chief citizen of the Republic. Addressed as Augustus ('the exalted one', a title hitherto reserved for gods), he inaugurated a new period of peace and prosperity, the 'pax Augusta', with a new form of government in which he, despite appearances, held all the reins of power. The Empire he had inherited as virtually sole ruler was destined to control the Mediterranean world from *c.*30 BCE to the end of the fifth century CE. Within its confines, Christianity rose (cf. Lk. 2:1) and spread, until by the first part of the fourth century CE it came, under Constantine, to be recognized as the state religion.

The Roman emperors of the New Testament period should be noted, and can be briefly summarized. After the death of Augustus in 14 CE, Augustus' adopted son, Tiberius, took over (at the age of fifty-six) and reigned until 37 CE. It was under his reign that Pontius Pilate was installed as procurator (26 CE). Tiberius was, in general, conscientious and efficient but he became neurotic about the loyalty of his subjects, and his final years were marred by a number of political trials ('treason trials'). The Prefect of the Praetorian Guard, Sejanus, one of the few he could trust, exerted great power and influence with Tiberius, and is considered to be the promoter of a number of the anti-Jewish policies associated with his reign. Pontius Pilate is reckoned by some scholars to have been Sejanus' protégé and his treatment of the Jews (as reported by Josephus, the Jewish historian) may have had the backing of Sejanus. Sejanus himself fell in 31 CE, a fact that some have considered significant in light of Pontius Pilate's vacillation over the trial of Jesus. He might have felt insecure, in the Emperor's eyes, it is conjectured, after the fall of his mentor (cf. 'If you release this man, you are not Caesar's friend', Jn 19:12).

Gaius Caligula, the son of Germanicus, Tiberius' adopted son and nephew, succeeded Tiberius in 37 CE. Caligula was only twenty-five years old at the start of what was to prove a very brief reign (37–41 CE). A capricious despot, he courted divine honours, and, among other things, attempted to place a statue of himself in the Jerusalem Temple, a plan only thwarted by his untimely death. Some have seen a veiled reference to this sacrilegious act in Mark chapter 13, verse 14. Caligula's uncle, Claudius, the conqueror of Britain (43 CE), took over from him (41–54 CE), and his imperial power impinges upon the New Testament when, according to the Roman historian, Suetonius, he expelled Jews from Rome (*c.*50 CE) 'at the instigation of one Chrestus' (could this be 'Christus'?; cf. Acts 18:1).

The most famous emperor of the New Testament period, of course, was Nero, the great nephew, stepson and adopted son of Claudius. He it was who initiated the first major officially sanctioned Roman persecution against the Christians (Tacitus, *Annals*, XV.44). Reference will be made to this later. Nero's relatively lengthy reign (54–68 CE) ended in civil war (68–69 CE), with no less than four contenders (Galba, Otho, Vitellius and Vespasian) battling for supremacy, and the right to occupy the imperial throne, when Nero died. That battle was won by Vespasian, thereby creating a Flavian dynasty which replaced the Julii and Claudii families of the previous emperors. Vespasian (69–79 CE) established a stable administration, renewed the principate initiated by Augustus and, where the New Testament is concerned, superintended the overthrow of the Jewish state, after the disastrous Romano-Jewish War of 66–73 CE.

Vespasian was succeeded by his two sons, Titus (79–81 CE.) and Domitian (81–96 CE), the former's exploits in taking Jerusalem and presiding over the destruction of its Temple being recounted by Josephus, but his brother, Domitian, had a more effective and enduring reign, although he faced numerous frontier problems along the Danube and the Rhine as well as with the Parthians in the east. Sadistic and given to megalomania, his rule became increasingly oppressive as he, too, like Nero, courted divine honours. The Revelation of John is seen by many as a response to the persecution inflicted on Christians in his reign. Both brothers may in fact be alluded to in the enigmatic description of the Beast with seven heads in Revelation chapter 17, verses 9–11, the seventh head being Titus ('when he comes he must remain only a little while', 17:10) and the 'beast that was and is not', Nero *redivivus* in the form of Domitian ('it is an eighth but it belongs to the seven and it goes to perdition', 17:11).

Nerva (96–98 CE), an old man adopted by the Senate to replace Domitian, was the first in a line of enlightened emperors, who sought to rule in correspondence with the ideas of Greek philosophy (cf. e.g. Marcus Aurelius, 161–180 CE). He was succeeded by Trajan (98–117 CE) who restored Roman fortunes in the troublesome frontiers, and whose correspondence with the governor of Bithynia, Pliny the Younger (111–113 CE), which I shall refer to later, reflects a Roman's view of a nascent Christianity suffering persecution in Asia Minor. The two last emperors of the New Testament period, Hadrian (117–138 CE) and Antoninus Pius (138–161 CE), are known to history as the 'wall-builders' of Britain, although, as far as the Jews were concerned (as we shall see in the next section), Hadrian was also a great destroyer of walls, the walls of Jerusalem, to be precise, in the disastrous Second Revolt (132–135 CE).

The social structure of Roman society was essentially a pyramid with Senate members and their families at the top, knights or equestrians beneath them, and the majority of Roman citizens or plebeians at the bottom. In addition, there were freedmen (ex-slaves who were normally non-citizens). At the base of the pyramid were the slaves, and at its pinnacle, over all, as *princeps*, was the chief citizen, the Emperor. The political structure of the Roman Empire was related to this and consisted of the Emperor at the head, with his council, the heads of government departments (procurators), the administrators of Rome and the provinces (prefects and proconsuls) and various other officials. There were two types of province: the public (or senatorial) province and the imperial province. Public provinces were governed by the Senate through proconsuls. Imperial provinces were ones that were usually militarily insecure and in which, therefore, the greater part of the army was stationed. In the first century CE between twenty-five and twenty-eight legions were under arms (at full complement a legion's strength was six thousand men and officers, plus an equal number of auxiliary troops). Imperial provinces, as the name implies, were ruled by the Emperor himself through his governors. These imperial provinces (and their governors) were variously named depending on the extent or nature of the troops stationed there (some provinces had one or more legions, others a single legion, others auxiliary troops alone). It was mainly to administer these provinces that Augustus established the equestrian class. Although directly responsible for the imperial provinces, the Emperor was also given power to intervene in public provinces. For parts of the Empire not thought ready or suitable for direct administration, the Romans governed via 'client kingdoms' ruled by friendly local potentates (Flerod the Great, for example, was one of these).

Another mainstay of the Empire was Roman law, which was highly developed. Well in advance of Christianity's influence, and in part as a result of Stoic philosophy (which we shall shortly turn to), the Roman legal system had introduced improvements in the status of women and the welfare of slaves. Punishment for public crimes, however, was severe, and consisted of crucifixion, beheading, burning alive, drowning and exposure to wild beasts. It was the right of any Roman citizen who was charged on a criminal matter to appeal directly to Caesar. The apostle Paul is described as doing this in Acts chapters 22 and 25ff. Roman citizenship was a coveted possession, and deemed a great privilege in the ancient world. It was often secured by the path of military service in the auxiliary forces.

Reference has already been made to the *pax Augusta*, or the *pax romana*, as it is often called. Under Roman rule, the material quality of life had improved for the Empire's peoples. A flourishing trade existed throughout the Empire, its citizens accustomed to a wide variety of goods and products, whether wheat and papyrus from Egypt, marble from Greece, or perfume, spices, gems, ivory, pearls, silk and slaves from India and the Orient. Communications were good, as the second-century bishop of Lyons, Irenaeus, testified: '[T]hrough their instrumentality the world is at peace, and we walk on the highways without fear, and sail where we will' (*Adv. Haer.* iv.30.3).[2] Roadmaking was the genius of the Romans, although brigands or highwaymen still constituted a problem for some travellers, as the parable of the good Samaritan indicates (Lk. 10:30–37). Though suspended during the winter months on account of storms, sailing was another important means of transport, and a major achievement of the Empire in the first century CE was to clear the sea of pirates.

To pay for the benefits of the *pax romana*, the Empire's peoples were subject to taxation. Various taxes were imposed, including the *tributum*, a direct tax (on land or personal property), which was levied on all who lived outside Italy (cf. Mk 12:13–17). The rights to collect these taxes were often sold to 'publicans' (*publicani*) who formed companies with shareholders in Rome and elsewhere. Although control of these companies was vested in procurators, abuses were common. To determine the tax base for the *tributum* and other taxes, local censuses were taken. After the deposition of Archelaus in 6 CE, for example, when Judaea reverted to direct Roman rule, Quirinius, the Roman commander in Syria, ordered a general census to be taken in Syria and Palestine (cf. Josephus, *Ant.* XVII.355; XVIII.1–10, 26). It may be a confusion with this particular census, which caused much protest, that lies behind the datum of Luke chapter 2, verse 1 that in the period of Quirinius' governorship, a general 'decree went out from Caesar Augustus that all the world should be enrolled'. Nothing, in fact, is known of a census at this time that was Empire-wide, and logically as well as logistically the idea is nonsensical.

The Empire also had a uniform system of coinage which served in addition the propaganda purposes of the Roman emperors. From 44 BCE onwards, when the Senate first authorized coins to bear the likeness of the ruler, the practice was adopted by successive emperors. Performing a role similar to today's postage stamps, these often had political, religious or military symbols on the obverse side (cf. Mk 12:13–17).

Although welcomed by the majority of European, Mediterranean and Middle Eastern peoples,[3] the *pax romana* was not viewed with entirely unmixed feelings by the Empire's subjects. For one thing, it was never completely unified, since there were a number of rebellions throughout the Empire at various times, and numerous mutinies on the part of troops. Rome's response to these was often brutal and merciless. In Calgacus' famous words in respect of the Caledonian campaign: 'To plunder, butcher, steal, these things they misname empire. They make a desolation and they call it peace' (Tacitus, *Agric.*, XXX).[4] Rome was not always true to her image as a tolerant power and some of the peoples or communities of the Empire feared and hated her oppressive rule, a good example being the Jewish–Christian community of Asia Minor from which the Revelation of John emerged.

The Hellenistic background

Having said something about the first of the three political and cultural backgrounds which make up 'the World of the New Testament', the Roman Empire, let me now turn to the second, the background supplied by Greek language and civilization, or 'Hellenism'. Here, I wish to concentrate on the cultural, social, philosophical and religious features of the Hellenistic world that have relevance for the New Testament. In speaking, moreover, of the Hellenistic background to the New Testament, I shall be making, by necessity, a number of general, and perhaps overly sweeping observations.

The catalyst for Hellenism, Alexander the Great, died in 323 BCE, but the vast Empire created by him did not survive his death. Politically, it disintegrated, with Hellenistic kings taking over Syria (the Seleucid dynasty) and Egypt (the Ptolemaic dynasty). Culturally, however, it survived and throughout the Mediterranean world Greek ways were being taken over and imitated. Greek culture was aped, appropriated, and coveted by all, and the Romans were no exception. When they took power in the Mediterranean world, they took over Greek architecture, Greek education, Greek science, and even the Greek 'gods' whom they identified with their own. The world was divided into Greeks and 'barbarians' (so-called, pejoratively, from the 'bar-bar' or indistinct noise or language deemed to be spoken by non-Greeks).

The Greek language became the *lingua franca* of the Roman Empire, its official language. Latin was used in the western provinces, however, and nothing was done to suppress the use of native languages (cf. Acts 14:11; 21:37). The Greek adopted was not classical Greek but *koine* ('common' or 'mixed'), and it is in this language that the religious texts of the New Testament are written. One testimony to the widespread use of Greek is the fact that when Paul, a Jew, wrote to the Romans, he wrote to them in Greek, and not Latin!

The Hellenistic age produced a panoply of distinguished poets and historians (some of whom have been previously mentioned): Virgil, Horace, Ovid, Livy, Nicholas of Damascus, Strabo, Seneca, Musonius Rufus, Pliny the Elder, Philo, Josephus, Tacitus, Suetonius, Martial, Juvenal, Dio Chrysostom, Plutarch, Epictetus, etc. It is worth pointing out, moreover, in relation to this literature, that the New Testament, while Jewish in origin, nevertheless has its rightful place within the extensive realm of Greek literature, in its Hellenistic phase.

Greek science, too, was taken over by the Romans, but its progress was often retarded by the influence of the theological and philosophical systems and ideologies that dominated the ancient world. We shall consider these in a moment, but first let me say something about the social background. The climate of the earlier part of the Hellenistic Age was rationalistic and sceptical. Man was the 'measure of all things', and the old 'gods' were seen as projections on a cosmic screen of human values (or the lack of them – the old 'gods' were often an immoral or disreputable lot!). Thereafter, in Gilbert Murray's famous and much repeated phrase, there was something of a 'failure of nerve' (i.e. before Rome established its Empire *c.*30 BCE and created order). Upheaval, unrest, uncertainty, a search for security in a changing world, confusion, turmoil – all these have been taken to characterize the latter part of the age. By the time of the birth of the New Testament, the tide of rationalism and scepticism had turned. The educated minority were taking refuge in philosophy, the lower classes in astrology, magic and superstition. There was a return to religion and to the 'new' gods sweeping in from the East. The New Testament era, then, was one of religious and cultural pluralism summed up in the apostle Paul's words in 1 Corinthians chapter 8, verse 5: 'There are many "gods" and many "lords"'.

Commentators often stress the immorality of the Hellenistic period, especially of the first century Roman world, and Hollywood epics like *Quo Vadis* or *Caligula*, with their uncomplimentary representation of Roman emperors, have done much to reinforce the popular image. Neither abortion nor the abandonment of infants was forbidden, and homosexuality (over which our own society is so divided) was sanctioned, and openly practised. Slavery was an accepted part of the system. Sexual promiscuity was widespread, especially on the part of emancipated Roman women. On the other hand, the kind of statistics on which we might base judgements on sexual practice, family matters, divorce rates, etc. are scanty for the ancient world. We often have to rely on the works of the Roman satirists (Musonius Rufus, Seneca, etc.) who frequently described extreme cases. Some of these moralists, moreover, were confirmed misogynists!

One response to the rootlessness of the age, the social disorientation or malaise, expressed itself in the number of voluntary groups that existed where people shared the same function, trade, profession or religion. Among them were associations termed *collegia*. The members of these *collegia* met to protect their common interests (e.g. the professional *collegia*), to worship the same deity (the religious *collegia*) or, in the case of the poor, to provide for welfare facilities and burial rights, as well as for fellowship (one might compare, in this respect, the nineteenth-century Friendly Societies). Although they were more inclusive socially than most Graeco-Roman *collegia*, from a sociological point of view, early church communities reveal a number of characteristics which resemble these distinctive Hellenistic associations.

If we turn to the philosophical background, then five philosophical schools dominated the age: neo-Platonism, Pythagoreanism, the Epicureans, the Cynics and the Stoics, the last three being particularly pre-eminent. The philosophy of Plato, the teacher of Alexander the Great, was influential at the beginning of the Hellenistic age, but had lost ground by the first century BCE. Plato's thought had been rehabilitated, however, under the influence of Plotinus, and the influence of Platonic ways of thinking is to be seen in writers such as the Alexandrian Jew, Philo, or in the New Testament in the Epistle to the Hebrews. Platonism distinguished two worlds: the first, the ideal world of perfect forms or ideas; the second, the shadowy world of earthly existence, which is no more than a pale reflection of this upper, purer, more spiritual world. This 'two world' dualistic notion permeates the philosophical and religious thinking of the age.

The teaching of the sixth-century philosopher, Pythagoras, mathematician, miracle-worker and sophist – also experienced a revival from the first century BCE onwards. One of its main protagonists in the late Hellenistic period was Apollonius of Tyana, an itinerant philosopher–magician, who practised asceticism, urged people to honour the gods and care for their temples, and, like Jesus, was accredited with numerous healing and nature miracles, including exorcisms and even a return from the dead.

The founder of Epicureanism was Epicurus. For him, the supreme goal in life was 'pleasure' by which he meant 'the absence of pain'. Epicurus advocated the virtue of *ataraxia*, i.e. impassiveness. He advocated the quiet life, withdrawal from the public, the cultivation of serenity. The community, he asserted, had no rights or claims over the individual, nor had the gods (who were to be treated with indifference rather than fear). Each person had to preserve his or her own peace of mind if fulfilment was to be achieved. Epicureanism was governed by Democritus' philosophy of 'atomism', i.e. the theory that everything is a 'fortuitous concourse of atoms'. The soul dissolves at death, and hence there is no afterlife for a man or woman to dread. What mattered in the end was this life.

If the 'pleasure' principle motivated the Epicureans, then the same cannot be said for the Cynics. Cynics stressed the worthlessness of all conventional standards. Virtue, they maintained, consisted in one's capacity to reduce one's needs to a minimum. The most famous Cynic was Diogenes who is said to have lived in a barrel! Like the Stoics, Cynics were itinerant 'street' preachers. They issued moralistic attacks on society which had a set form, the 'diatribe'. This form is reflected in the New Testament writings (e.g. in the Pauline Epistles or the Letter of James). Links between early Christians and Cynics have recently been maintained, some scholars arguing that first-century marketplace audiences would have found little to distinguish between the message brought by Cynic preachers and that proclaimed by Christian missionaries. Some (e.g. F. G. Downing) have even claimed that Jesus was a Jewish Cynic, the often acerbic social teaching found in the Gospels bearing striking similarities to that promulgated by this philosophical school.[5]

Milder in this respect were the Stoics, a movement founded by Zeno of Citium (*c.*336–263 BCE). Other famous Stoics were Cleanthes, Chrysippus and Posidonius. Stoicism underwent many transformations and had a capacity to mix its philosophy with much mythology or superstition, a fact that accounted, some say, for its popularity. Stoicism saw the world as a unity or as a body whose soul, spirit, ordering principle, creative mind, intelligence – call it what you like – was God, the *Logos* (a supreme being also identified with Zeus). The divine *Logos* had many manifestations and could split into many creative spiritual forces. Man (the ancient world was not as gender-sensitive as we are today!), by virtue of his reason, participated in the divine *Logos*.

Man can rise above his circumstances, the Stoics maintained, and be fulfilled, if he lives his life according to 'reason'/*logos*, and this was interpreted as living according to nature, which reflected the divine *Logos*. All human life, especially as organized into society, should be governed by these laws of nature that reflect in turn the divine Intelligence. By virtue of *logos*, or indwelling 'reason', all men were equal, an emphasis which proved attractive to the citizens of the Hellenistic world, given their predilection for cosmopolitanism. A high moral tone (if somewhat austere) was also adopted by the Stoics, and correspondences between their teaching and that of the New Testament writers have been detected in a number of passages (cf. e.g. Acts 17:28; Rom. 1:19–23, 11:36, 13:1–7; 1 Cor. 7:17–24, 8:6; Col. 3:18–4:1; Eph. 4:6; Jas 3:1–5).

If philosophy was the refuge of the upper and middle classes, then religion dominated the lower classes. Greek religion, the official religion of ancient Greece, was civil and corporate, communal not personal. Worship was demanded of the old gods (the gods of Homer and the Greek tragedians), the gods of Olympus, at stated times and on formal occasions at which set rites or ceremonies were performed. The purpose of these rites was to secure the favour of the gods on the community and the Empire. Not to participate was seen as an anti-social, even anti-patriotic act. Worship of these old gods declined, however, in the Hellenistic period, and for three main reasons: first, many were purely local deities associated with a particular locale (e.g. Artemis or Diana at Ephesus; Athena at Athens); second, attacks on their morals had been launched by Greek writers (e.g. Plato, Euripides, Xenophanes, Euhemerus) and, third, the mythology surrounding them was no longer meaningful and was often found unadaptable to new circumstances, especially by the middle classes.

One prominent form of civil religion in the ancient world did flourish, however, namely, the imperial cult. The cult promoted the practice of worshipping the Emperor as a deity. Although adopted reluctantly in the West, it was common practice in the eastern provinces. In Italy and in Rome, sacrifice was made to the 'genius' of the Emperor, and not to the Emperor himself – Rome was uncomfortable with living 'gods' in its midst. In the West, emperors were usually only deified after their death. In the provinces, however, sacrifice was 'to Rome and Augustus'. Taken over from the worship accorded to Hellenistic kings, especially in Asia Minor, the cult was found convenient, for political reasons, by Roman emperors. Organized, with priests, it was carefully controlled by them. It was only Jews and Christians who did not participate in the cult, special concessions having been granted to the former. Christians, however (when they came to be identified separately as such), excited charges ranging from lack of patriotism to atheism because of their non-participation, and drew official suspicion or even persecution or native pogroms as a result. A highly colourful and strongly condemnatory response to the cult can be seen in the last book of the New Testament, the Apocalypse or Revelation of John.

The Hellenistic age saw the influx of many new gods and cults, e.g. those dedicated to Asclepius, or to Dionysus. Asclepius was the god of healing, and the temples built to him were the hospitals of the ancient world. The cult of Dionysus (or Bacchus, as he was known to the Romans) emanated from the region of Thrace and/or Phrygia and was an orgiastic, life-confirming cult, with an emphasis on drama and ecstasy. Dionysus (like Jesus in the Fourth Gospel) was the god who could turn water into wine. Although not widely popular, Orphism, with its stress on sin and guilt, and on salvation through purification and holy living, also drew a number of adherents.

A key phenomenon of the Hellenistic age was what scholars have called syncretism. Syncretism means the identification of one god or goddess with another, and is hence marked by the fusing of names and attributes. The tendency, as a result, was towards monotheism, the one 'supreme God' or deity. A remarkable example of this occurs in Apuleius' *Metamorphoses* (or *The Golden Ass*)[6] where Isis announces herself to the hero Lucius with the words:

> I am she that is the natural mother of all things, mistress and governess of all the elements, the initial progeny of worlds . . . manifested alone and under one form of all the gods and goddesses. . . . [M]y name, my divinity is adored throughout all the world in divers manners, in variable customs, and by many names. For the Phrygians . . . call me the Mother of the gods at Pessinus; the Athenians . . . Cecropian Minerva; the Cyprians . . . Paphian Venus; the Cretans . . . Dictynnian Diana; the Sicilians . . . Proserpine; the Eleusians . . . Ceres; some Juno . . . Bellona . . . Hecate . . . Rhamnusia . . . and the Egyptians . . . call me by my true name, Queen Isis (XI. 5).

The Hellenistic age saw in particular the influx of a number of esoteric cults or 'mystery religions' from the Orient, cults that worshipped 'dying and rising gods', saviour-figures, union with whom brought salvation from fate or death. The precursors of such rites were those celebrated in connection with Demeter at Eleusis. There were three main cults in particular: the cult of Isis and Osiris from Egypt; the cult of Cybele, the Great Mother Goddess from Asia Minor; and the cult of Mithras from Persia. Though a certain amount of mystery still surrounds them, these cults had certain general characteristics. They tended to offer highly emotional, dramatic rites in which the initiate was led to experience mystical union with the god and hence rebirth to new life. They practised baptism or ritual lustration, and shared sacred meals. They also had some special characteristics. The cults of Isis and the Great Mother were public cults, with itinerant, mendicant priests. The cult of Isis and Osiris, which was often spread by sailors, had its 'madonna and child', the mother goddess being depicted in figurines with the infant Horus on her knee. Mithraism, a rival to Christianity from the second century CE onwards, was a private cult, popular with soldiers, and celebrated in an (often underground) temple or *mithraeum*.[7] The bull was a symbol of Mithras, and the god's birthday was celebrated on 25 December, the winter solstice. Where the Christian believers of the Revelation of John had their robes washed in the blood of a lamb (Rev. 7:14), the initiate to Mithraism (in the ritual of the *taurobolium*) was washed in the blood of a bull.

The Hellenistic age was a credulous one. Magic and super-stition were rife. The popularity of magical practice is evidenced in many quarters: in the classical writers, in extant magical papyri, in the New Testament itself, and in the writings of the later church fathers. Stories and legends circulated about the exploits of numerous wonder-workers and magicians, both Hellenistic and Jewish: Simon Magus, Apollonius of Tyana, Rabbi Hanina ben Dosa, Jesus of Nazareth. Augury (the examination of entrails) was practised. Many illnesses or diseases were viewed as the product of demon-possession, and tales of exorcism were popular in the period.[8] Even certain of the Roman emperors were cred-ited with miracle-working powers.[9]

Fatalism was widespread in the Hellenistic age, the belief that the world was unresponsive to human effort or merit. Everything changed in response to blind 'Chance' or inexorable 'Fate'. People's fortunes were, like everything else, in a constant state of flux. In consequence, the desire to find some ground of certainty was a dominant motivation behind popular response to the new religious movements and cults. Astralism, too, was popular, the belief that humankind's fate lay in the stars, human destiny being governed by the heavenly bodies, or rather the gods or powers that presided over them (and which were usually seen as malignant). Astrologers wielded great influence over the emperors.

One phenomenon of the Hellenistic age that placed great emphasis on the gods or powers presiding over the heavenly spheres surrounding the earth was Gnosticism. Gnosticism was once seen as a second-century CE Hellenistic formation, a Christian heresy resulting from the radical Hellenization of Christianity (A. Harnack),[10] a product of the influence of Greek thought on the Jewish–Christian tradition. Gnostic ideas, however, are now believed to have been circulating in the first-century CE world, and perhaps even before. For Gnostics, the world was seen as evil and under the power of an evil god or Satan. God himself was a transcendent being, living in a realm beyond the spheres. Certain individuals (the elect) have in them a 'divine spark'. Between God and the evil world, and proceeding from him are a series of emanations or *aeons*. According to one myth, one of these, the Gnostic Redeemer, descends to earth to call the elect to a heavenly ascent to their true home by revealing to them the 'knowledge' (*gnosis*) by which the journey is made possible (hence the name 'Gnostic'). Such ideas may have been influential in the formation of Christian belief. The Fourth Gospel, for example, was deemed by R. Bultmann to be the religious product of a Gnostic Redeemer myth, although this view is not taken as seriously by contemporary scholarship as it once was.

What was Rome's attitude to these new religious movements? They called them *superstitiones*, and the cult of Christianity, of course, was numbered among them. Tolerant in so many other respects, the Romans displayed contempt for the East and for these exotic cults. They challenged, after all, formal Roman religion and its traditional values. They undermined family life, devotion to the old gods, the household gods, the Lares and the Penates (the gods of hearth and home). They undermined loyalty to Rome, the Empire and the Emperor. They encouraged, it was believed, various forms of immorality (e.g. sexual promiscuity, ritual murder, infanticide, incest, cannibalism). A number, as a result, were suppressed at various times: the cult of Dionysus (the Bacchanalia), the Druids, the Isis cult. Persecution for the Christians emerged only, however, when this new religious movement began to be seen as distinct from its mother-religion of Judaism. Before this, being considered a Jewish movement, with a Jewish background, it enjoyed, in Roman eyes, the privileges of a permitted religion, a *religio licita*.

The Jewish background

In sketching out the third of our three backgrounds to early Christianity and the New Testament world, namely, the Jewish background,[11] let me first give a brief summary of the main historical and political events in relation to the Jewish nation which both preceded and ran concurrently with the origins of the Jesus movement, early Christianity and the emergence of the New Testament writings. In Table 1 (opposite), I have listed some key political leaders, events, dates and periods, and you might like to refer to this. Some, like the Roman emperors, have been mentioned already.

In the course of their history, the Jews were dominated by successive world empires. They were defeated by the Babylonians in 586 BCE, Jerusalem was destroyed and they were carried off into exile, so creating communities of the 'dispersion' or *diaspora*. The Babylonians were in turn succeeded by the Persians (538–332 BCE). They proved more benevolent where the Jews were concerned, particularly to those who had returned to their homeland. The empire of Alexander the Great (332–323 BCE) followed the Persians but after Alexander's death that empire disintegrated, as previously mentioned. Three main dynasties emerged: that of the Antigonids in Macedonia (who are not important for our purposes), that of the Ptolemies in Egypt (323–198 BCE) and that of the Seleucids in Syria (198–142 BCE). Rome became the next major Mediterranean power, intervening for the first time in Jewish political affairs in Palestine in the year 63 BCE. With the reign of Augustus (27 BCE–14 CE), the Roman Empire consolidated itself.

Until the Seleucids, Jews had relative autonomy in religious matters. Thereafter they experienced forced Hellenization,

Table 1 Leaders, events, dates and periods

Alexander the Great	332–323 BCE
The Ptolemaic Dynasty (Egypt)	323–198 BCE
The Seleucid Dynasty (Syria)	198–142 BCE
Antiochus Epiphanes	175–165 BCE
The Maccabean/Hasmonean periods	142–63 BCE
The Roman Period	63 BCE onwards
Augustus	27 BCE–14 CE
Herod the Great	37–4 BCE
Archelaus	4 BCE–6 CE
Philip	4 BCE–34 CE
Herod Antipas	4 BCE–39 CE
Judas of Galilee and the Revolt	6 CE
The Period of the Roman Procurators	6 CE onwards
Tiberius	14–37 CE
Pontius Pilate	27–37 CE
Gaius Caligula	37–41 CE
Herod Agrippa I	41–44 CE
Claudius	41–54 CE
Nero	54–68 CE
The Romano-Jewish War	66–73 CE
Vespasian	69–79 CE
Titus	79–81 CE
The Fall of Jerusalem	70 CE
Johanan ben Zakkai and National Reconstruction	70 CE onwards
Domitian	81–96 CE
Council of Jamnia	90 CE (?)
Nerva	96–98 CE
Trajan	98–117 CE
Hadrian	117–135 CE
Bar Kokhba and the Second Revolt	132–135 CE

especially under Antiochus Epiphanes (175–165 BCE). Sacrifice to their God, Yahweh, was prohibited, the eating of pork was enforced (contrary to their food laws) and circumcision (a major identity marker) was banned. An altar to Olympian Zeus was set up in the Jerusalem Temple, an act of such gross sacrilege that this 'abomination of desolation' was to inspire the first major apocalyptic writing (the book of Daniel) and to become a nightmarish feature of later Jewish visions of the end of the world. Some factions within Jewry welcomed Hellenism, but others fiercely resisted, in particular a group of pious Jews called the *Hasidim*. The origin of the later Jewish sects (the Pharisees, Essenes, Sadducees) is dated by many scholars to this time.

In response to these attacks upon their religious practice and identity, the Jews revolted. The revolt was led by a priestly family, the House of Hasmon (who later founded the Hasmonean dynasty), in particular by a priest called Mattathias who had five sons. The eldest, Judas Maccabaeus ('the hammer') conducted guerrilla warfare against the Seleucids, was successful and in 164 BCE restored Temple worship. The Jewish Feast or Festival of Hannukah ('Lights') celebrates this event. The Jews, as a result, had a period of relative independence which lasted from 142–63 BCE.

Factionalism between two descendants of the Hasmoneans led, however, to Roman intervention, in the shape of Pompey, and Rome gained a foothold in Jewish affairs which it never again lost. This was especially the case when Herod, a half-Jew from Idumaea, succeeded in establishing himself as king of the Jews in 37 BCE. Herod the Great was in fact a vassal king, the puppet of one of the Romans' client kingdoms. Herod is known as a brutal tyrant, one associated with the abolition of Jewish civil rights. On the other hand, it should be said, he presided over an era of unprecedented prosperity – although he bled the population with taxes to achieve it. Herod promoted Hellenistic culture: the building of Greek temples, cities and arenas, and the introduction of Greek games at which participants performed nude, thus offending Jewish sensibilities. He also reconstructed the Temple, although he blotted his copybook by erecting a golden eagle (symbol of Rome) over the doorway. This incident gave rise to a revolt on the part of the Pharisees and the Essenes, an uprising which was nevertheless ruthlessly suppressed.

After his death, Herod's kingdom was divided among his three sons. Philip took the north-eastern part of the kingdom, and reigned as tetrarch between 4 BCE and 34 CE. Antipas took Galilee and Peraea, and reigned as tetrarch until 39 CE. Archelaus presided over Judaea, Samaria and Idumaea, but only for ten years, until 6 CE. Archelaus proved as insensitive as his father had been. When satisfaction was demanded by the Jews in respect of the 'golden eagle' incident, Archelaus had the demonstrators massacred. It was during this period, Josephus tells us, that a variety of Messianic pretenders arose to challenge him. Archelaus was eventually deposed by the Romans, and Judaea virtually became an imperial province, i.e. (you may recall) one directly ruled by procurators responsible to the Emperor. In Judaea's case, however, it was placed under the aegis of the larger province to the north, Syria. As a result, Quirinius, the governor of Syria, instituted a census for taxation purposes in 6 CE (cf. Lk. 2:1), with Coponius being sent to oversee it. Reference has already been made to this. The census led to another revolt, however, this time at the hands of a Judas of Galilee (or Gamala) in alliance with a certain Sadduk, a priest. According to a popular body of opinion, Judas was the founder of the movement known as the Zealots or Sicarii ('assassins'). The Romans, who kept their troops head-quartered in Caesarea (Maritima), and not in Jerusalem (except for a contingent in the Antonia fortress), responded, in their usual brutal and efficient manner, by putting this revolt down.

Under the Emperor Tiberius (14–37 CE), Judaea was governed, as noted above, by the procurator Pontius Pilate (27–37 CE). After Tiberius' death, the despotic Gaius Caligula took over and threatened to disturb Romano-Jewish relations further by erecting a statue to himself as Zeus in the Jerusalem Temple (40 CE). The Jews, however, found an ally in Petronius, the legate of Syria, who temporized, and with Caligula's death in 41 CE, the crisis was averted. For a brief period thereafter, Judaea became a client kingdom again with the appointment of Herod's grandson,

Herod Agrippa I (41–44 CE). He it was who persecuted the primitive Christian church, according to Acts chapter 12, verses 1–3 and 21–23. After his early death, the region, nevertheless, reverted to the Romans, although his son Agrippa II was given north-eastern Palestine as well as the right to oversee the Temple (cf. Acts 25:13).

A succession of relatively bad or inept procurators ensued: Cuspius Fadus, Tiberius Alexander, Ventidius Cumanus, Felix (cf. Acts 24), Festus (cf. Acts 24 and 25), Gessius Florus and Albinus. One of the factors leading to this situation was a reversal of Tiberius' erstwhile policy of placing procurators in the province for a reasonable time. The subsequent short-term policy adopted had the effect of encouraging ambitious men to use the province as a stepping-stone to better appointments. Romano-Jewish relations inevitably worsened, leading to the First Jewish Revolt and a disastrous war (66–73 CE). Events came to a head when the Jews refused to offer sacrifices on behalf of the Emperor. The resulting conflict led to the destruction of the city, and the burning of the Temple, a cataclysm graphically described by Josephus in his *Jewish War* (see note 13).

After the fall of Jerusalem in 70 CE, and the demise of the foremost Jewish institution, the Temple, national reconstruction began. The Torah and the synagogue became the rallying point. A new Jewish centre was established at Jamnia (Jabneh). The leadership of the nation passed to prominent rabbis such as Johanan ben Zakkai. The Sanhedrin, the highest Jewish council, was now composed of Pharisees and scribes, the high priestly families who had hitherto held the reins of power having been killed or having fled during the war. Some of their traditions and influence was preserved at priestly schools set up, in opposition to Jamnia, at Lydda and Sepphoris in Galilee. Although the former Temple tax paid by all Jews was now paid into Roman coffers, the hope of Temple restoration was also kept alive between 70 and 135 CE when the next great Jewish upheaval occurred.

In the time of Hadrian, the Jews received a promise that the Jerusalem Temple would be rebuilt. The failure of this promise led to the (so-called) Second Revolt. This period saw the advent of a man of heroic proportions, Simon bar Kosiba, or Bar Kokhba, as he was nicknamed, the 'son of a star' (cf. Num. 24:17; ' a star. . . come forth from Jacob, a sceptre . . . rise out of Israel'). Bar Kokhba was acclaimed by the renowned Rabbi Akiba. The period was one of considerable eschatological ('end-time') fervour. Most Jews enlisted in the cause, with the exception of Jewish Christians who, according to the Church father, Justin Martyr,[12] were persecuted for their allegiance to another Messiah. The war with Rome led to another inevitable defeat. Jerusalem was razed to the ground, and renamed Aelia Capitolina. A temple to Jupiter was erected on the site, and it became a Gentile city. Golgotha (already a Christian site of pilgrimage) was obliterated and replaced by a statue to Aphrodite. The Jews were expelled from their former city, and prohibited from re-entering. Only in the fourth century CE were they thereafter allowed to do so, and then only on one day a year, the 9th Ab (end of July/beginning of August), by way of commemoration.

As this brief history indicates, relations between the Jews and the Romans were somewhat turbulent. After 70 CE, Jews were definitely *personae non gratae* in Roman eyes. Relations had in fact been deteriorating from the forties, although earlier they had in general been good. By virtue of rights secured under Julius Caesar and Augustus, Judaism, as already noted, was a recognized religion with a legal status, a *religio licita*. Among other things, Jews were exempt from military service, and were not required to attend court on a sabbath. Their right to collect the Temple tax from their Diaspora communities and despatch it to Jerusalem had been safeguarded, at least until the fall of the city in 70 CE. They had been excused from participation in the imperial cult, being allowed instead to offer prayers on behalf of the Emperor in their synagogues, and sacrifice on behalf of, but not to, the

Emperor in their temple. Such sacrifices (which ceased, as we have seen, in 66 CE) were even paid for from imperial funds. Roman standards (*signa*), which were regarded by the Jews as idols, were usually left outside Jerusalem, the one prominent contravention of this (under Pontius Pilate who, under cover of darkness, introduced effigies of the Emperor into the city, *BJ* II.169–174) leading to a riot which led to their removal.[13] Jews were allowed to be citizens of other cities without losing their Jewish nationality (under Roman law no one could be a citizen of two cities). Christians, too, remained under this umbrella as long as they were considered a Jewish sect, and so in the early days they suffered from their fellow Jews, and not from Rome.

Where political administration in Palestine was concerned, the Roman procurator had limited functions. He did not rule like a king, and so provincial status was welcomed by many Jews. When it came in 6 CE, the change of government had little impact on the masses. Jewish autonomy was preserved, to a certain extent, through the high priest and the Sanhedrin, or Jewish council. Under vassal kings like Herod the Great, the high priesthood had nominal power, but under direct Roman rule, the high priest was the primary political head (even although a number of them were deposed). The high priest was head over the Sanhedrin whose membership included the high priestly families, scribes of the Pharisees and Sadducees who were experts in legal tradition and interpretation (to be discussed shortly) and wealthy upper-class Jewish aristocrats called elders. The Sanhedrin was the supreme legislative, judicial and administrative authority, although it had no right of capital punishment (this was vested in the procurator), and therefore no power to execute offenders except for desecration of the Temple (cf. *BJ* VI. 125; Acts 21:26–30).[14]

In Palestine, economic circumstances for the Jewish masses were modest, if not downright poor. Jews were doubly taxed. They were taxed by the civil power, and they were taxed by the religious authorities. Only upper-class Jerusalemites or major landlords in Galilee were wealthy. A substantial Gentile minority lived in Galilee, and many of these landlords were non-Jewish, therefore, and absentee landlords to boot. The major occupations were farming (carried out principally on the northern plains and in the vicinity of Jerusalem), fishing (on the Sea of Galilee), handicrafts and small businesses. Jewish artisans made their living as fullers (laundrymen), weavers, tailors, smiths, carpenters, potters, or, if they were educated in the Law, as scribes. Some occupations were despised, such as tanning (which involved impure contact with dead animals) or tax collection (which involved a different form of impurity, namely, collaboration with the Romans). For peasants, life was hard labour, and the rewards few. A number of tradesmen, artisans and peasants found employment in connection with Herod the Great's numerous building programmes, the construction of the Jerusalem Temple being one, but poverty and unemployment ensued for many when this prodigious edifice was completed in the early sixties. Brigandage was rife, as the parable of the good Samaritan again illustrates (Lk. 10:30–37). Many Jews emigrated to join their Diaspora cousins elsewhere. Of the estimated four and a half to seven million Jews in the first century, only a fraction lived in Palestine. There were major Jewish centres in Cyrene, Alexandria (two of its five districts were Jewish), Rome, Antioch and Ephesus.

The social life of the Palestinian Jew revolved around the family, whose structure was patriarchal. The father was the breadwinner, and he it was who instructed his sons in the Law. The Jewish male was allowed the sole right to divorce, the Mosaic Law (cf. Deut. 24:1) having given him the power to dissolve his marriage with a letter witnessed and signed by two other men only. A marriage sum had to be raised and given to the divorced wife, however, and a fresh sum had to be raised for the next marriage dowry. The grounds for divorce were debated, particularly between the liberal and conservative schools of Hillel and Shammai.

The position of women was an inferior one. Women were banned from the inner Court of the Temple, and had to remain within the Women's Court reserved for them. No active participation, it seems, was allowed in synagogue worship. Their role was only to listen. While they had to observe the prohibitions of the Law, they were not required to keep all of the commandments nor to study the Law (and hence become truly educated). Their status has been well summed up in the famous words of the second-century CE Rabbi Judah who urged three thanksgivings on his fellow Jews:

> Blessed be He who did not make me a Gentile.
> Blessed be He who did not make me a woman.
> Blessed be He who did not make me an uneducated person (Tosefta Berakhot VII.18).[15]

Slaves, it should be said, received better treatment under the Jews than among other communities of the Hellenistic world. Hence, many of them became converts to the faith or proselytes. According to the Jewish Law, a slave had to be released by his master in the sabbath year, that is, not more than seven years after captivity. In reality, there were very few slaves in Palestine since not many were rich enough to own them. Jewish slaves of Gentile masters, moreover, were often quickly bought out of slavery, or 'redeemed', by other Jews.

Despite this colourful, at times tragic history, and these inauspicious political, economic and social circumstances, the Jews of Palestine and the wider Mediterranean world managed to create and preserve a distinctive cultural and religious heritage. The language of the Palestinian Jew was Aramaic (a form of Hebrew) as well as Greek, that of the Diaspora Jew almost exclusively Greek. In the Diaspora itself, there was widespread use of a Greek translation of the Hebrew Bible, the Septuagint (LXX). The word means 'seventy' and it derives from the tradition that as seventy elders received the Law originally with Moses (cf. Exod. 24:1, 9), so seventy were responsible for its translation. *The Letter of Aristeas* (late second century BCE) offers a different version, claiming that seventy-two were responsible, six from each of the twelve tribes. The translation was probably made in Alexandria by the mid-third century BCE, although some would dispute this.

Jewish non-canonical literature of the pre-and post-Christian period can be divided into five main categories. The first of these is what is termed the 'Apocrypha'. The Apocrypha are the 'hidden, secret, esoteric' books. They comprise some fourteen or fifteen books in all, and are additions to the Septuagint which were rejected from the Hebrew canon by the rabbis at the Council of Jamnia (*c.* 90 CE) but approved for private study or edification. In terms of genre, they comprise books of history, romantic tales, wisdom literature and apocalyptic works. They bear such names as 1 and 2 Esdras, Tobit, Judith, Additions to Daniel or Esther, 1 and 2 Maccabees.

The second category is the 'Pseudepigrapha'. These are the 'false writings', i.e. the books published under an assumed name. They were decisively rejected by the rabbis, and are not even in the Septuagint. In terms of genre, they are mostly apocalypses, hence their rejection by the rabbis who were rightly wary of a genre of writing which could be said to have inflamed the situation that had led to the disastrous Romano-Jewish War and subsequent Jewish misfortune. They bear such names as the Psalms of Solomon, The Testament of the Twelve Patriarchs, the Book of Jubilees, the Book of Enoch, 2 Enoch or the Book of the Secrets of Enoch, the Assumption of Moses, the Martyrdom of Isaiah, the Apocalypse of Ezra, the Apocalypse of Baruch.

The third important category is that of the Dead Sea Scrolls. These scrolls are the literature of the Qumran community, a community now widely assumed to be identical to the Essenes, on whom we shall comment shortly. Discovered in the Judaean desert and brought to the attention of scholars in the 1950s, this diverse library of writings, in Aramaic, Hebrew and Greek, presents a number of rules (e.g. the *Community Rule* which gives an account of the sect's aims and purposes and initiation rites, or the *War Rule*, which prepares its members for eschatological battle with its enemies), poetic, liturgical and wisdom texts (e.g. hymns of thanksgiving, blessings, curses, exhortations, etc.), biblical interpretation (e.g. commentaries, including *pesharim*, i.e. expositions of prophecy with a contemporary slant; testaments, i.e. farewell or deathbed speeches which anticipate the future; targums, i.e. vernacular scripture paraphrases, testimonia or catenae, i.e. groups of texts selected to reinforce a particular theme; and midrash, i.e. imaginative or fanciful expositions or interpretations of scripture, etc.) and miscellaneous material (e.g. *The Copper Scroll*, which records hidden treasures!).

A fourth category is the literature of Rabbinic Judaism itself. When we speak of the literature of Rabbinic Judaism, we mean the literature of the Judaism which was normative after 70 CE, a Judaism which was influenced by the Pharisees who were in their ascendancy then. Rabbinic Judaism produced two main bodies of texts in particular, the Mishnah and the Talmud. The Mishnah represented the codification of the oral law which had grown up around the Torah, the first five books of Moses. It contains legal interpretations of that law, otherwise known as *halakhah*. It was largely compiled by a generation of rabbis called the Tannaim, and completed somewhere around 200 CE. The written Mishnah attracted further commentary (*Gemara*), and the subsequent combination of the Mishnah with the Gemara produced the Talmud. The Talmud contains legal exposition, argument, rulings, as the Mishnah had done before it (*halakhah*), but it incorporated in addition material that was edificatory (*haggadah*). This *haggadah* consists of parables, prayers, miracle-stories, legends, allegories and meditations. It was compiled by a generation of scholars called the Amoraim between the third century and the end of the fifth century CE. There were two versions of it, the Palestinian Talmud, completed around 350 CE, and the Babylonian Talmud, which was completed around 500 CE.

Our final category of Jewish literature is the literature of Hellenistic Judaism, i.e. the literature of the more liberal Judaism of the Diaspora. This consists, among other things, of the writings of Josephus, and the Jewish philosopher-theologian Philo, both of the same century as Jesus. Flavius Josephus (37/38–post 100 CE) was a Palestinian Jew who, despite being a revolutionary commander in Galilee during the Jewish Revolt, rose to prominence in imperial court circles by virtue of his self-serving support of Vespasian. A stout defender of his Jewish ancestry and heritage, as well as of all things Roman, he produced one of the most valuable records of the period for anyone interested in the Roman Empire in the Judaeo-Christian period. His works include a lengthy account of the Romano-Jewish War in seven books (*The Jewish War*), an even lengthier account of the history of the Jews in twenty books (*The Antiquities of the Jews*), as well as some other more minor works (*The Life, Against Apion*).

Philo (*c.*30 BCE–50 CE) was a native of Alexandria, the premier Hellenistic city of the ancient world, and a member of one of its wealthiest Jewish families. The leader of a delegation to Gaius Caligula to plead for the Emperor not to pursue policies inimical to his Jewish countrymen, Philo was an ardent supporter of both Judaism and Hellenism. Like Josephus, he wrote extensively and with a concern to represent his Jewish heritage in terms of the Greek philosophical tradition to which he was also an heir. His works include philosophical writings, treatises which offer allegorical and homiletical expositions of scripture, or treatments of Old Testament laws, biographies and other historical works. Influenced by the Greek philosophical schools, his prodigious literary output offers Judaism with a Platonic or Stoic slant. Like the author of the Fourth Gospel, he made much of the Stoic concept of the *Logos* as an intermediate being. His *Life of Moses* presents Judaism's most famous hero, not only as a gifted law-giver and general but also as a divine man in keeping with Hellenistic conceptions.

Having summarized the various categories of Jewish literature which throw light on the world of the New Testament, let us now turn to the religious background. Although they often overlap, four main types of religious tradition can be detected in ancient Jewish life, literature and experience: the cultic tradition, the prophetic tradition, the apocalyptic tradition and the legal tradition.

The first of these, the cultic tradition, has as its principal institution the Temple. The key operative agent, or functionary, of this institution is the priest (or to a lesser extent, the Levite). The dominant religious emphasis in this tradition is social, ritualistic or liturgical. Stress is laid on the importance of observing the various rites connected with the Temple, including the regular festivals or feasts. Where salvation is concerned, man's access to God is obtained through observance of the sacrifices which ensured national and spiritual well-being for the community. In relation to Jewish religious literature, Old Testament (or Hebrew Bible) books such as Leviticus or Deuteronomy reflect this tradition.

The second main tradition in Jewish experience is the prophetic tradition. Here, the principal institution is not the Temple but the old or new covenants. Here, the key operative agent of the tradition is not the priest but the prophet or mystic. While it may be individual or national, the religious emphasis of this tradition tends to be moral and anti-cultic. Where salvation is concerned, God's contact with humankind comes in the events of history, particularly in a future judgement, or coming day of the Lord. A human being can be God's agent, and a prophet his inspired mouthpiece. The prophetic writings in the Old Testament (or Hebrew Bible) reflect this tradition (e.g. Isaiah, Jeremiah, Hosea, Joel, Amos, etc.).

The third main tradition in Jewish experience arises out of the prophetic one, namely the apocalyptic tradition. Here, there is no principal institution since the tradition is forward-looking. The key operative agent is the end-time prophet, the apocalyptic visionary, or even the Messiah. The emphasis in this tradition is eschatological, i.e. it looks to the end of the present world and to the coming of the new. God is remote and transcendent, and salvation will come about only by his supernatural intervention in the coming age, at which time a new heaven and a new earth will be created. The dominant tone, then, of apocalyptic is pessimistic, this world being seen as evil and under the domination of Satan, and hence no longer the arena, as for the prophet, of God's redeeming activity. In relation to the Jewish literature which we have reviewed, it is the Pseudepigrapha and a number of writings among the Dead Sea Scrolls which provide a window into this important tradition.

Our final main tradition is the legal one. Here, the principal institutions are the Torah, the synagogue and to an extent the sabbath. The key operative agent is the scribe, whose function it is to interpret as well as transmit the law. The dominant emphasis of this tradition is hence a legal one. For the protagonists of this tradition, it is only a faithful observance of the daily prescriptions of the law that will secure salvation. The Mishnah and the Talmud are the religious texts in which this attitude is to be seen in its most developed form.

With these simple (but not, we hope, simplistic) categories in mind, we turn finally to the four principal sects of Judaism at the time of Jesus: the Sadducees, Zealots, Essenes and Pharisees. All four are mentioned by Josephus, three originating from 'ancient times', he claims, the fourth (now widely identified as the Zealots) of more recent origin:

> The Jews, from the most ancient times, had three philosophies pertaining to their traditions, that of the Essenes, that of the Sadducees, and, thirdly, that of the group called the Pharisees . . . As for the fourth of the philosophies, Judas the Galilean set

himself up as leader of it. This school agrees in all other respects
with the opinions of the Pharisees, except that they have a
passion for liberty that is almost unconquerable (Ant. XVIII. 11,
23; cf. also BJ II.119).[16]

The Sadducees are (probably) named from Zadok, chief priest
under David and Solomon (2 Sam. 8:17; 1 Kgs 2:35), whose
descendants claimed the right to rule Israel. Several groups
claimed legitimate descent from Zadok in the Maccabean Revolt.
One group retired to Qumran. Another retained control in
cooperation with the Hasmoneans and became the Sadducees.
A patrician party comprising members of the high priestly
families, the landed aristocracy and other wealthy individuals,
the Sadducees were the most prominent sectarian group before
the fall of Jerusalem in 70 CE. Known to us from Josephus, the
New Testament and Rabbinic sources, they were the conservative element in Israel. Believing in free will and resisting all forms
of determinism, they advocated individual responsibility together
with loyalty to the state, the Temple and the Jewish law. They
rejected innovations to the Jewish law intended to accommodate
it to changing times or circumstances. They rejected doctrinal
innovations (if there was no basis for them in the Torah), for
example, resurrection of the dead, the apocalyptic intervention
of God with supernatural salvation and final judgement, angels
and demons. Salvation was achieved through strict adherence
to the law. Proper worship was that accorded to God in the
Temple. Maintaining cooperative relations with the Empire, and
hence seen as collaborators, they were in the end unable to avert
the disastrous war with Rome (66–73 CE) which resulted not
only in the destruction of the Jewish state but also in their own
demise. They can be taken as exemplars, therefore, of the cultic
(in part legal) religion that we have already outlined.

Our next group, the Zealots, were pitted against the Sadducees.
As commonly understood, the Zealots were a first-century

religio-political party characterized by its zeal for the one true God, a desire for the autonomy of the land of Israel (*eretz Israel*), a stubborn refusal to submit to Rome (in the spirit of Maccabean resistance to foreign domination), and a willingness to suffer for its beliefs. The New Testament makes little mention of them, although links with Jesus have been suggested (cf. e.g. his association with Simon 'the Zealot', Lk. 6:15; his 'cleansing' of the Temple, his death by crucifixion). Jewish history abounds with 'zealots', activists who, in their 'zeal' for the God of Israel, believed themselves to be his agents for judgement or liberation (cf. e.g. Phinehas, Num. 25:6–18, whose chief claim to fame rests upon his having driven a spear through a fellow Israelite and his offending Midianite partner, thereby placating Israel's God and averting a plague). As an identifiable and unified revolutionary movement, however, the nature, history and origins of the 'Zealots' are much debated. In consequence of Josephus' ambiguous references to them (as 'brigands', 'the fourth philosophy', *Sicarii* or 'dagger-men', 'Zealots'), some claim that they were a definite sect with a history stretching back to the Maccabees (W. R. Farmer, *Maccabees, Zealots and Josephus*), others that they originated at the time of the census protest in 6 CE under Judas of Galilee, others still that they did not emerge until 67–68 CE and even then were only one of a number of rebel factions prosecuting the war. Whether Jewish resistance to Rome was indeed engineered by them, or whether it resulted from sporadic, spontaneous and unconnected popular outbursts of anti-Roman feeling is a matter of controversy, but many would still claim Judas as the founder of the sect, and accord it a considerable degree of influence in the revolutionary struggle. Whatever their precise origins, however, they may be taken as exemplars of prophetic (and to an extent apocalyptic) religion.

Known from Pliny the Elder, Philo and Josephus, the Essenes (who also lived in city communes) were now generally regarded as identical with the community that produced the Dead Sea Scrolls.

The word 'Essenes' means the 'pious ones'. They were descendants of the *Hasidim* (the 'pious ones') who remained loyal to Jewish tradition in the face of their enforced Hellenization by the Syrians in the early second century BCE. The Essenes claimed descent from Zadok too and opposed the attempt of the Maccabean rulers to usurp high priestly office without priestly descent. A Hasmonean/Sadducee coalition defeated the Essenes, however, and, led by a certain 'teacher of righteousness' and in opposition to a 'wicked priest', they retired to the desert 'to prepare the way of the Lord' (cf. Isa. 40:3 and IQS VIII.12–16). The Essenes claimed that the Temple authorities and worship were illegitimate and the masses of Israel therefore impure. They were the true Israel, setting themselves apart for holiness and purity and awaiting the day when God would send his Messiah(s) to lead them against the *Kittim* (Romans), to restore the Temple and priesthood, to execute judgement on their enemies, and to inaugurate the new age. Unmentioned in the New Testament – although some claim John the Baptist as an Essene – the sect offers numerous parallels to the beliefs and practices of early Christianity (e.g. in its eschatology, Messianic expectation, sense of election, use of scripture, worship, common meals, baptismal practice and attitudes to the Temple, marriage, wealth and the sharing of goods), as well as major differences (e.g. its exclusivism, hierarchical structure, strict attitude to the law, emphasis on ritual purity, sabbath observance and celibacy). In common with the Sadducees, they advocated strict adherence to the Torah, but in contrast to their rivals, they trusted to divine intervention rather than to individual initiative. They practised quietism in the present, but at the same time urged military preparedness for eschatological battle. Trusting to divine intervention, they disappeared in 68 CE, destroyed, it appears, in the fearsome advance of the Roman armies. They may, therefore, be taken as exemplars of the apocalyptic (and to an extent cultic) religion I have described.

Surviving the catastrophe, the Pharisees (meaning, it is suggested, the 'separatist' people set apart for obedience to God) gained ascendancy after 70 CE, becoming leaders of the synagogue and opponents of early Christianity. Despite the confusing picture presented by our sources, it seems clear that they were progressive in their attitude to religion and innovative in their doctrine. Accepting a wide body of Jewish scripture as authoritative, and appropriating from Hellenistic and oriental culture ideas not found in the Torah (e.g. eschatology, apocalypticism and Messianism), they entertained belief in angels and demons, life after death, final judgement and resurrection of the dead. In this respect, they had little in common with their arch-rivals, the Sadducees, and much with Jesus and his followers. Exhibiting in legal matters both a liberal (the 'house' of Hillel) as well as a conservative wing (the 'house' of Shammai), they emphasized the importance of the oral and written law, and with it the need for ritual purity and tithing. Lay scholars rather than priests, they attempted to apply the laws of Temple purity to everyday life, promoting thereby (to use a 'Protestant' expression) the 'priesthood of all believers'. Although separated in religious terms from the '*am ha' aretz* or 'people of the land', they exhibited in political affairs a democratic tendency, frequently emerging as protectors of the people's rights versus the government. Some Pharisees espoused political Messianism or apocalypticism. Most saw themselves, however, as a religious sect devoted to the Law rather than a political party (though the question of their relation to politics is debated). They may be taken, therefore, as the exemplars of legal religion, as outlined above.

Reference above to the '*am ha' aretz* is a salutary reminder that, in discussing Jewish sects, it is easy to overlook the fact that the majority of Jews lived their lives without affiliation to any sectarian movement. Part of a largely poor, rural, peasant or artisan class, with little time, inclination or resources to appreciate the intricacies of theological doctrine or to observe the minutiae of religious practice, the average Jew was in the main only indirectly affected by Jewish sectarianism. Most Palestinian Jews lived in small villages rather than in the wealthier urban centres of the Hellenistic period. The term *'am ha' aretz* itself has a variety of geographical, political, socio-economic or religious connotations. In the Old Testament (or Hebrew Bible) it referred either to the native population, to non-Jews living in the Jewish homeland, to the common people as opposed to kings, royal officials or priests, or to the property-owning and politically influential (male) citizenry of a specific territory, as opposed to either the upper echelons or the lower strata of society. In the Rabbinic literature, it referred to those who did not observe the Jewish law (especially the laws of ritual purity) as opposed to the Pharisees or rabbis, and thus became a term of abuse for those regarded as lax or ignorant in matters of morality or religion. It is with such people, the 'sinners', that Jesus is said to have freely associated, hence giving rise to Pharisaic criticism of him.

★ ★ ★

The world of the New Testament, then, is a fascinating world, both rich and diverse. It is, as we have seen, the world of the Roman Empire, the world of Greek language and civilization, the world of Jewish religion and culture. It was a world of unprecedented peace and prosperity, yet one punctuated by upheaval, unrest and uncertainty. It was a world of new philosophies and new religions which challenged the old order and the old gods. It was a world that believed in supernatural intervention in the affairs of humanity, in demon-possession, in angels and gods who visited humankind for good or ill, in portents that heralded the significant events in human life, the birth and death of its significant citizens and heroes. It was a world that accepted miracles as normal rather than paranormal, in life after death or resurrection of the dead, in the advent of a new age in which humankind's cares would be wiped out with the arrival of a new heaven and a new earth. In this age, men and women were offered a variety of philosophies and religions, a host of philosophers, magicians, exorcists, saviour-figures, prophets, priests and gods who would bring them varying degrees of health or salvation.

The citizen of the first-century CE world could adopt the philosophy of neo-Platonism, or that of the Pythagoreans, the Epicureans, the Cynics or the Stoics. He or she could join the new cults, those of Asclepius, or Dionysus or that of Orphism, or become initiates of the mystery religions of Isis, Cybele or Mithras. If a Jew, he or she could embrace cultic religion, worshipping or offering sacrifices in the Temple or attending the great Jewish feasts. He (less so she) could throw in his lot with the Zealots to fight for national liberation from the Romans. He could retire, on the other hand, from political or national life to lead a monastic life as an Essene, awaiting God's supernatural intervention in history, his sending of the Messiah, the dawn of the apocalyptic age, the restored Temple, the new heaven and the new earth. Alternatively, he could take on the yoke of the law, and become a Pharisee, devoted to the practice and observance of the Torah in the daily round of life. This is the world of the New Testament, and it is in the context of this world, its needs and aspirations, its hopes and fears, its world-view (or world-views), that the birth of Christianity must be viewed.

2
The early church

The origins and history of the early church

Having explored the world of the New Testament in the first chapter, let me now turn to the community (or communities) of the New Testament, or the 'early church'. By the 'early church', I mean the church in the New Testament period, i.e. between the death of Jesus, *c*.30 CE, to the date of the last writing to be included in the New Testament canon, 2 Peter, usually dated not later than *c*.150 CE. I shall also be using another term, the 'primitive church' or the *Urgemeinde* (the 'primal community'), the Jerusalem church, or the church in the period between 30 and 70 CE, comprising the first Jewish followers of Jesus and their leaders.

The sources for our knowledge of the early church may be divided into two categories, namely, the non-Christian sources and the Christian ones. Among the former are the Graeco-Roman historians or the Jewish sources. Among the latter are the so-called church fathers, the non-canonical writings (i.e. those outside the New Testament) and the canonical writings of the New Testament itself.[17]

The Graeco-Roman sources consist of the writings of such historians as Tacitus, governor of Asia *c*.112 CE; Suetonius, the private secretary to Hadrian; his friend Pliny the Younger, a barrister; Sulpicius Severus, another barrister; and Dio Cassius, consul in 211 and 229 CE. Some of these have been referred to already. Tacitus (*c*.60–120 CE) wrote a work called the *Annals*,[18] from which the following excerpt on the Neronian persecution is taken:

But all human efforts, all the lavish gifts of the emperor, and the propitiations of the gods, did not banish the sinister belief that the conflagration was the result of an order. Consequently, to get rid of the report, Nero fastened the guilt and inflicted the most exquisite tortures on a class hated for their abominations, called Christians by the populace. Christus, from whom the name had its origin, suffered the extreme penalty during the reign of Tiberius at the hands of one of our procurators, Pontius Pilatus, and a deadly superstition, thus checked for the moment, again broke out not only in Judaea, the first source of the evil, but also in the City, where all things hideous and shameful from every part of the world meet and become popular. Accordingly, an arrest was first made of all who confessed; then, upon their information, an immense multitude was convicted, not so much of the crime of arson, as of hatred of the human race. Mockery of every sort was added to their deaths. Covered with the skins of beasts, they were torn by dogs and perished, or were nailed to crosses, or were doomed to the flames. These served to illuminate the night when daylight failed. Nero had thrown open his gardens for the spectacle, and was exhibiting a show in the circus, while he mingled with the people in the dress of a charioteer or drove about in a chariot. Hence, even for criminals who deserved extreme and exemplary punishment, there arose a feeling of compassion; for it was not, as it seemed, for the public good, but to glut one man's cruelty, that they were being destroyed (XV.44.2–8).

Suetonius (*c*.75–160 CE) also makes reference in his *Life of Nero*[19] to this infamous event:

Punishment was inflicted on the Christians, a class of men given to a new and wicked superstition (XVI.2).

He, too, like Tacitus, regarded Christians as scum, as this excerpt indicates.

Another key passage on the early church is that contained in the correspondence between the Emperor Trajan and Pliny the Younger (62–*c*.113 CE),[20] a correspondence which took place when Pliny was governor of Bithynia, in Asia Minor, and which was occasioned by his seeking the advice of the Emperor on how to deal with the troublesome Christian sect. These references are meagre, however, since Christianity did not come to the particular attention of the Romans until a period later than the apostolic one.

Another important source is that of Josephus, who, as we have seen, wrote *The Antiquities of the Jews* and *The Jewish War*. In *Ant*. XVIII.116–119 and XVIII.63–64, he refers to John the Baptist and Jesus respectively (the latter passage is known as the *Testimonium Flavianum*), and in *Ant*. XX.197–203 he gives an account of the death of James, brother of Jesus, in 62 CE. There is little else about the church. A Slavonic version of Josephus, the so-called Slavonic Additions to *The Jewish War* (Book II), does refer to Christians, however, as well as to John the Baptist and Jesus, but these Slavonic Additions are undoubtedly the work of later Christians.[21] Subsequent tampering by Christian scribes makes the Josephan evidence untrustworthy, however, although some credibility is given by scholars to the John the Baptist material, and a narrow consensus of scholarly opinion would probably favour some element of authenticity in the *Testimonium Flavianum*. Other Jewish sources reflect the conflict between Christians and Jews which led, among other things, to the banning of Jewish Christians from the synagogue in the latter half of the century. These sources have little value, however, for the pre-70 CE period.[22]

The first category of Christian sources is the Church fathers. Among those who give us traditions about the early church are Clement of Rome (whose *First Epistle to the Corinthians* is dated *c*.96 CE), Justin Martyr (who died 165 CE), Eusebius of Caesarea (264–349 CE), whose *Ecclesiastical History* spans four centuries from the foundation of the church to Constantine,[23] and Epiphanius (*c*.315–403 CE). The fathers write considerably later than the events they purport to describe, however. They draw on legends or traditions which are often not easy to verify, and their views on Christian origins, in addition, are often influenced by their own doctrinal or ecclesiastical concerns or prejudices.

The non-canonical writings consist, among other things, of various Apocryphal Gospels with titles such as the Gospel of the Nazoreans, the Gospel of the Ebionites, the Gospel of the Egyptians, the Gospel of Peter, and the Gospel of Thomas. By far the most important of the non-canonical Gospels to have been discovered in the last century is the Gospel of Thomas. This is a key text in current studies of Christian origins and the historical Jesus. Some, like the Gospel of the Ebionites, or the Gospel of the Hebrews, are Jewish–Christian, and may preserve traditions that go back in some part to the early Jewish–Christian church. On the other hand, these non-canonical Gospels also contain material that is obviously later, secondary and manifestly inauthentic. The majority of these writings do not survive, moreover, in their entirety. Often they are only known to us through quotations or allusions (frequently tendentious) in the writings of the church fathers. The evidence they offer is difficult, therefore, to assess. It is unlikely that they are earlier than our canonical Gospels. Some would place their composition from the beginning of the second century onwards.

Our main sources, therefore, are the New Testament writings, especially (Luke–)Acts, the Pauline Letters and the Gospels. Other New Testament writings, namely the Deutero-Pauline Letters (e.g. the Pastoral Epistles) and the Catholic Epistles (with the possible exception of the Epistle to the Hebrews and the Letter of James), were written too late to supply us with data concerning the first two generations of the church. Our main sources have to be treated with caution, however. There are discrepancies between Paul and the Acts of the Apostles. The Acts and the Gospels present not history but theologically interpreted history or tradition. They often reflect not the church situation in the apostolic period but that pertaining in the period when they were written, that is after 70 CE in the sub-apostolic period. In the (so-called) Acts of the Apostles, there is in fact comparatively little data about the original twelve. Hence, we must be alive to the three levels at which data may in fact be offered in the writings: some material may possibly go back to the earliest period or stratum (level 1); some data may have been modified, altered, embellished or invented by the church in the oral period when its traditions were being circulated (level 2); some elements may be due to the early Christian writers themselves (level 3). Having said this, let us now turn to the picture of Christian origins presented by the Gospels, the Acts of the Apostles and Paul.

In the Gospels, Jesus is presented as the proclaimer of the coming kingdom of God. He directed his hearers to God and his imminent, supernatural intervention in history. The content of his message was the rapidly approaching advent of the Messianic age, God's coming rule. In Acts, as in Paul, the early church is found directing people, by contrast, to Jesus, not the coming kingdom. The content of the church's message, in other words, is Jesus himself. In R. Bultmann's famous words, 'the Proclaimer became the Proclaimed' in the experience of the early church.

In a famous book appearing in the 1930s, *The Apostolic Preaching and its Developments*, the British scholar, C. H. Dodd, listed what he thought were the rudiments of early Christian preaching, as uncovered from the speeches attributed to Peter in the Acts of the Apostles (and as confirmed by the writings of Paul). The outline of the typical apostolic sermon, he claimed,[24] was as follows:

1. The Messianic Age has dawned, in fulfilment of all the prophecies about it.
2. This has taken place through the ministry, death and resurrection of Jesus, in accordance with the divine foreknowledge and deliberate purpose of God.

3. By virtue of his resurrection, Jesus has been exalted at the right hand of God, as Messianic head of the new Israel.
4. The Holy Spirit in the church is the sign of Christ's present power and glory.
5. The Messianic Age will shortly reach its consummation in the return of Christ (the technical term is *parousia* = royal visit).
6. An appeal ends the *kerygma* (or proclamation), with forgiveness, the Holy Spirit, and a promise of salvation (viewed as participation in the life of the age to come) being offered to those who repent and accept the *kerygma*.

Few scholars nowadays would agree with Dodd that there was one uniform primitive *kerygma* which conformed to this pattern and which is consistently reflected in the New Testament writings. Contemporary scholars prefer to talk of the various *kerygmata* or proclamations about the status and activity of Jesus (who he was, what he did) that were entertained by the early Christian communities and which produced our New Testament writings. Nevertheless, there is a substantial agreement (especially in European, though less so in North American scholarship), that the message of the primitive Jewish–Christian communities was *eschatological*, i.e. that it concerned the end of the present world order and the beginning of the new. The belief was entertained by such communities, moreover, that Jesus would shortly be returning to earth as judge and saviour (the *parousia*). Primitive Christianity was a Jewish sect, therefore, which finds its origin or ground in that form of Jewish religion or tradition that we typified in chapter 1 as prophetic or apocalyptic. In contrast to the other Jewish sects that entertained apocalyptic expectations, it claimed that Jesus was the promised Messiah and that the Messianic Age had dawned. Jesus was not a failed Messianic pretender, although he had been crucified by the Romans. Jesus' Messiahship had been vindicated by his resurrection, and the Messianic Age was about to be consummated by his *parousia*, when judgement and blessing would be dispensed to non-believer and believer alike.

This belief was strong not only in the early church but at certain other times in the church's history, for example, at the time of the Neronian persecution, or a little later during the Romano-Jewish War, when Mark's Gospel is thought to have been written, or at the time of the Emperor Domitian (when the Revelation of John was likely to have been produced), or of Trajan (when 1 Peter was probably composed). History refuted eschatology, nevertheless. Jesus did not return in the lifetime of the early Christians. The church had to adjust, therefore, to this refutation of one of the fundamental claims of its original *kerygma*. The various ways in which this adjustment was made are reflected in the writings of the New Testament, texts which were produced at different times and in different circumstances during a period of over a hundred years. In his *The New Testament. Proclamation and Parenesis Myth and History* (1994), N. Perrin outlines three particular strategies which were adopted:[25]

1. The stubborn reiteration of the claim despite the passage of time (cf. e.g. 2 Peter, in all likelihood the New Testament's final writing, especially 2 Pet. 3:3–13).
2. The extension of the *eschaton*, or end-time events so that they occur within a broader timescale, and the theological justification for the interim period so created (cf. Luke–Acts).
3. The reinterpretation of the belief, the *eschaton* being deemed to have occurred in the cross, and the *parousia* through the giving of the Spirit (cf. the Fourth Gospel).

As this example shows, the New Testament writings not only reflect a variety of theological emphases and adjustments made through time to the primitive *kerygma*, but they also bear the stamp of the various historical phases through which early Christianity passed. It is worth commenting on these phases, since the literature which was produced by the early church (and which we shall consider in chapter 3) has been influenced by historical developments that mark the distinctive evolution of early Christianity.

Scholars identify two basic periods, which it is convenient to differentiate. The first is the period between 30 and 70 CE, the period from the death of Jesus to the fall of Jerusalem. It is called the apostolic period (and we have referred to it as such already), or the 'tunnel' period, because so little is known about it. The second is the period from 70 to 135 CE, the period from the fall of Jerusalem to the Bar Kokhba Revolt, or to 150 CE, the approximate date of the last of the writings contained in our New Testament. This is called the post- or sub-apostolic period.

Scholars also identify three basic forms of early Christianity which correspond to the three historical phases through which New Testament Christianity is believed to have passed. The first is Palestinian–Jewish Christianity associated with the Palestinian–Jewish phase of Christianity's origin and spread. The second is Hellenistic–Jewish Christianity which is associated with the Hellenistic–Jewish phase. The third is Gentile Christianity associated with the Gentile phase.

Commentators frequently remark on the rapid expansion of Christianity in the first century CE from Palestine into the wider Hellenistic world. From Jerusalem, it spread to Alexandria in Egypt, to Antioch in Syria, to Ephesus in Asia Minor, to Corinth in Greece, and to Rome in Italy. According to N. Perrin, Jesus proclaimed the coming kingdom of God in Palestine in Aramaic and died, according to Mark chapter 15, verse 34, with the Aramaic version of Psalm 22, verse 1 on his lips ('My God, my God, why have you forsaken me!'). Twenty years later, however, the Christian message has moved from being proclaimed in Aramaic to being proclaimed in Greek. It has moved from Palestine itself into Europe. It has moved from the Jewish world into the wider Hellenistic world. It has passed from being a proclamation by Jesus about the coming kingdom of God to being a proclamation by the church about Jesus himself as that eschatological event.[26]

From the limited evidence available to us, we know that the primitive church, the *Urgemeinde*, was an apocalyptic sect with a strong eschatological emphasis and message. Its community consisted primarily of Jews who were on the whole conservative and law-observant. They practised a strict obedience to the Jewish law, including the observance of circumcision, the food laws and the sabbath, and they attended the Temple regularly. The main difference from their orthodox Jewish compatriots lay in their belief in Jesus' Messiahship and in his imminent *parousia*. They were preparing themselves for the coming day of the Lord. They did so through prayer and the communal sharing of goods. They appealed to their own countrymen to repent and prepare themselves for the new age predicted in the Hebrew Bible. In addition to his twelve disciples, the leaders of the *Urgemeinde*, or Jerusalem church, were members of Jesus' own family, his brother James, in the first instance, followed by his cousin Simeon who died in Trajan's reign. The succession, therefore, appears to have been a dynastic one. There is no evidence in this early period, moreover, of persecution as such from the Romans. The only sporadic persecution of the community seems to have come from fellow Jews (cf. e.g. Acts 8:1–2, 12:1–5).

As we saw in chapter 1, an attitude to Hellenism split Jews into 'liberal' and 'conservative' camps. It divided Jews into those who favoured or admired Greek institutions and thought (liberals) and those who saw Hellenism as undermining Jewish loyalty to institutions like the law, the Temple and ultimately to God himself (conservatives). The strict Palestinian Jew was often suspicious, therefore, of the Hellenistic Jew. The early Christian community was a community of Jews, and this basic division among Jews in general appears to have manifested itself among Jewish Christians in particular. Evidence suggests that there was internal conflict within the *Urgemeinde*. This conflict is associated with the names of Stephen and Paul. In Acts chapter 6, verse 1, there is an ambiguous reference to two groups within the *Urgemeinde*, the 'Hebrews' and the 'Hellenists'. The 'Hellenists' are widely interpreted as Greek-speaking 'liberal' Jewish-Christians within the primitive church, and the 'Hebrews' as Aramaic-speaking 'conservative' Jewish–Christians. Tradition attaches Hellenistic names to the seven leaders said to have been at the forefront of this Hellenistic wing of the Jerusalem church: Stephen, Philip, Prochorus, Nicanor, Timon, Parmenas, Nicolas. They denounced, it appears, what was deemed the narrow exclusivism of the conservatives, their rigid adherence to the law, and they claimed that the Temple cultus was unnecessary.

These denunciations drew a sharp response from conservative Jews in general. Stephen was stoned, and the Hellenistic wing of the church persecuted (cf. Acts 8:1–2). Conservative Jewish–Christians seem, however, to have escaped this persecution, including the leaders of the Jerusalem church (cf. Acts 8:1b, '*except the apostles*'). Further evidence suggests that this persecuted Hellenistic wing of the church was then responsible for carrying Jewish Christianity from Jerusalem into the wider Hellenistic world, first into Judaea and Samaria, then into the Diaspora. Their success among Hellenistic Jews, and among a group of non-Jews who admired Jewish ways and emulated them without becoming proselytes, namely those known as 'God-fearers', is documented in the Acts of the Apostles.

The spread of this 'liberalized' form of Jewish Christianity into the wider Hellenistic world brought it into more contact with Gentiles. Jewish Christianity was translated, some would say transformed, into terms acceptable to the Gentile world, and it found ready acceptance there. This was an effect which may indeed have set the original Palestinian followers of Jesus back on their heels, since their message was one directed in the main to their own fellow Jews. The chief missionary work in this area was that by a Hellenistic Jew called Saul of Tarsus, otherwise known to us as the apostle Paul. His Gentile mission, and the circumcision issue which it opened up, seems to have intensified the rift between the conservative wing of the *Urgemeinde* and the emergent Pauline wing. Paul's letters testify to the fact that he suffered much opposition to his brand of Christianity, and to his understanding of the significance of Jesus. Paul was attacked as a non-apostle and as one preaching a different gospel from that of the original disciples.

It must be stressed again that the evidence from this 'tunnel' period is admittedly uncertain. It suggests, however, that between 30 and the early 60s CE, the authority of the original Jerusalem church held sway (i.e. the authority of James and his conservative wing), and that this authority was regarded as normative. Paul was regarded, it seems, as somewhat of an upstart, his apostleship and authority something he had to defend continually. But after 70 CE, the situation changed dramatically. In this period, Gentile Christianity shows itself to be strong, assertive and flourishing while Jewish Christianity declines and almost fades into oblivion. The decline of Jewish Christianity and the ascendancy of Gentile Christianity in the post-apostolic period is so remarkable that one scholar at least (S. G. F. Brandon) has expressed the view that Christianity was effectively reborn after 70 CE.[27]

How is this phenomenon to be explained? What are the factors that led to the eclipse of Jewish Christianity and the influence of the *Urgemeinde?* One factor was undoubtedly the martyrdom of James, the brother of Jesus in 62 CE (cf. Josephus, *Ant.* XX.197–203 and Eusebius, *Eccl. Hist.* II.23). Another was the martyrdom of a number of the other leaders, such as James, the son of Zebedee (Acts 12:1–5) in the reign of Agrippa I, or Peter in the Neronian persecution in 64 CE. This was the time at which legend also places the martyrdom of Paul.[28]

Another potentially important tradition is that of the Jerusalem church's flight to the Gentile city of Pella at the outbreak of the Romano-Jewish War (cf. Eusebius, *Eccl. Hist.* III.5.3 as well as

Epiphanius). The *Urgemeinde's* flight from the Jewish capital would have effectively removed it, it has been argued, from the mainstream of Christian life, tradition and history, a stream which was henceforth to move in a Gentile direction. This tradition has been doubted, nevertheless, by some scholars (e.g. S. G. F. Brandon, G. Strecker, W. R. Farmer, J. Munck)[29] who maintain that the original Jewish Christians took common cause with their fellow countrymen, and died defending Jerusalem and its Temple from their Roman oppressors. If this were the case, then it too would provide a reason for the eclipse of Jewish Christianity.

Jewish Christianity did not die out completely, however. There is some evidence of its survival. Its influence exists in the Gospel of Matthew, for example, and in one of Matthew's sources, the 'sayings' source Q, which we will come to in due course. It exists also in the New Testament letter attributed to Jesus' brother, James. The survival of early Jewish-Christian tradition and belief can also possibly be seen in Jewish-Christian sects such as the Ebionites and the Nazoreans. These appeared in the second century, they claimed an origin from the *Urgemeinde*, and they regarded Paul as the perverter of the original message of Jesus. Not surprisingly, they were deemed heretical by the now orthodox Gentile-Christian communities. It was they who produced some of the Apocryphal Gospels earlier mentioned, as well as works such as the Pseudo-Clementines.

If such factors contributed to the eclipse of Jewish Christianity, what contributed to the ascendancy of Gentile Christianity? One obvious factor was the delay of the *parousia*. This delay led inevitably to a reinterpretation of eschatology and to a de-emphasis on the apocalyptic roots of the Jewish sectarian movement that was originally Christianity. The tendency was accelerated in the wider Hellenistic world, since Gentiles did not tend to think in these characteristically Jewish terms. Gentiles in the main did not understand apocalyptic or had little time for eschatological ideas. This tendency, moreover, was part and parcel of a more general movement in Gentile Christianity to de-emphasize its Jewish roots. Gentile Christians preferred not to present themselves as adherents of a Jewish sect with a crucified Messianic pretender as its founder, especially one about to return on the clouds of heaven, but as a universal religion worshipping a divine Lord or Son of God who had brought salvation to all humankind.

We observe, therefore, in the post-apostolic period, the growing influence, if not the rehabilitation of Pauline thought. Paul had been the 'apostle to the Gentiles' *par excellence*. The writings to the churches he had founded were gathered together (as many as could be found) to form the Pauline corpus in the New Testament. Many of these are composite, showing the fragmented nature of this collection in its original state. The historian–theologian known to us as 'Luke' also produced the first history of the church, the Acts of the Apostles, a work whose main actor, it should be noted, was the non-apostle Paul! Acts glosses over the internal conflicts that appear to have been a feature of the earlier period. It displays a distinct pro-Roman bias, and, among other things, has an apologetic function. It was designed to show the Roman world that it had nothing to fear from the growth of this new religion. And the very fact that a history of early Christianity could have been written at all is an indication of the waning of eschatological expectancy within this period!

These, then, are the formative factors which scholars have isolated as accounting for the development and spread of early Christianity and which were a feature of early Christian experi-ence: the phenomenon of persecution; the Hellenistic-Jewish and Gentile missions; the delay of the *parousia*; the eclipse of Jewish Christianity; the effect of the Romano-Jewish War; the ascendancy of Gentile Christianity. It is these factors, therefore, that must be held in mind in any analysis of the history of early Christianity and the emergence of its literature.

The nature and development of early Christian belief and practice

Having outlined the origins and history of the early church, let me now say something about the nature and development of early Christian belief and practice in the New Testament period. A good place to start is with an excerpt from one of the Graeco-Roman sources to which I referred above, namely, the correspondence between Pliny the Younger and the Emperor Trajan.[30] In his capacity as governor of Bithynia, and in pursuit of the Emperor's advice, Pliny describes his dealings with Christians, and, in so doing, reveals some interesting facts about the nature of Christian belief and practice in Asia Minor in the early years of the second century:

> It is my custom, lord emperor, to refer to you all questions whereof I am in doubt . . . In investigations of Christians I have never taken part . . . Meantime this is the course I have taken with those who were accused before me as Christians. I asked them whether they were Christians, and if they confessed I asked them a second and third time with threats of punishment. If they kept to it, I ordered them for execution; for I held no question that whatever it was that they admitted, in any case obstinacy and unbending perversity deserve to be punished. There were others of the like insanity; but as these were Roman citizens, I noted them down to be sent to Rome . . . As for those who said that they neither were nor ever had been Christians I thought it right to let them go, since they recited a prayer to the gods at my dictation, made supplication with incense and wine to your statue which I had ordered to be brought into court for the purpose together with the images of the gods, and moreover cursed Christ – things which (so it is said) those who are really Christians cannot be made to do. Others who were named by the informer said that they were Christians and then

denied it, explaining that they had been, but had ceased to be such, some three years ago, some a good many years, and a few even twenty. All these too both worshipped your statue and the images of the gods and cursed Christ.

They maintained, however, that the amount of their fault or error had been this, that it was their habit on a fixed day to assemble before daylight and recite by turns a form of words to Christ as a god; and that they bound themselves with an oath, not for any crime, but not to commit theft or robbery or adultery, not to break their word, and not to deny a deposit when demanded. After this was done, their custom was to depart, and to meet again to take food, but ordinary and harmless food; and even this (they said) they had given up doing after the issue of my edict, by which in accordance with your commands I had forbidden the existence of clubs. On this I considered it the more necessary to find out from two maid-servants who were called deaconesses, and that by torments, how far this was true: but I discovered nothing else than a perverse and extravagant superstition. I therefore adjourned the case and hastened to consult you. The matter seemed to me worth deliberation, especially on account of the number of those in danger; for many of all ages and every rank, and also of both sexes are brought into present or future danger. The contagion of that superstition has penetrated not the cities only, but villages and country; yet it seems possible to stop it and set it right (Pliny, *Letters*, X.96).

This passage offers us a Roman view of nascent or infant Christianity. It is seen as a secret society ('their habit. . . to assemble before daylight'). It was a banned organization, a *collegium illicitum* ('my edict, by which . . . I had forbidden the existence of clubs'). It is seen as a 'perverse and extravagant superstition'. The word 'perverse' hints at the cannibalism of which early Christians were accused ('to take food, but ordinary and harmless food'). The reference to the taking of an oath (*sacramentum*) to behave in certain prescribed ethical ways is an allusion perhaps to early Christian adoption of the Ten Commandments. One also notices that Pliny sees Christianity as a 'dangerous' contagion which appeals to all classes of people ('many of all ages and every rank and also of both sexes are brought into present or future danger'). There is an historical irony, too, in his expressed optimism that, where Christianity is concerned, 'it seems possible to stop it and set it right'! This is an outsider's view but it is valuable inasmuch as it gives us an external glimpse into the nature of early Christian belief, worship and institutions. It is to early Christian belief and practice that we now turn, but this time from the perspective of the insider.

Given the nature of this *Beginner's Guide*, it is impossible to treat the intricacies of Christian belief and practice in the New Testament in any appreciable detail. What I propose to do is to give an outline of the main features, to show how early Christian beliefs and practices developed during the New Testament period, and to identify particular trends. In treating Christian belief, first of all, the terminological map I shall be working with is one that has nine co-ordinates, namely theology, Christology, soteriology, pneumatology, cosmology, eschatology, anthropology, ecclesiology and ethics. These technical terms are familiar to systematic theologians. The New Testament writings, of course, do not articulate a uniform, formal or coherent system of belief, and are characterized by diversity, but these terms, once understood, offer, for our purposes, a convenient way of categorizing different aspects of early Christian religious thought within a short compass. A glossary of the terms is given in Table 2, overleaf, and you might like to refer to it in the ensuing discussion.

The term 'theology' comes from two Greek words, *theos* meaning 'God' and *logos* meaning 'word', or, by extension, 'teaching' or 'rational discourse'. In its narrow sense, a New Testament writer's 'theology' means his understanding or belief about God,

Table 2 The early church (belief)

Term	Meaning	From Greek
	Doctrine/teaching/ understanding of:	*logos* = doctrine, teaching,
Theology	God	'talk of'; *theos* = God
Christology	the Person of Christ	*Christos* = Christ
Soteriology	the Work of Christ	*soter* = saviour
		soteria = salvation
Pneumatology	the Spirit	*pneuma* = spirit
Cosmology	the World	*kosmos* = world, universe
Eschatology	the End of the World	*eschatos* = last, final
		eschaton = the end of the age
Anthropology	Man	*anthropos* = man
Ecclesiology	Church/Community	*ekklesia* = church, community of believers
Ethics	Relation of believer to Christ, fellow believers in the Church and fellow human beings	*ethos* = custom, usage *ethikos* = pertaining to morals

and this is how we shall use it. In its broader sense, of course, the word 'theology' refers to a whole complex of related subjects in Christian teaching, subsuming all of the other categories given here, and more besides. Christology (from *Christos* meaning 'Christ' or 'Messiah') is the word we shall use to describe the teaching or understanding found in a New Testament writer or writing concerning the person or nature of Christ, and, by contrast, soteriology (from *soteria* meaning 'salvation') the word for any teaching or understanding concerning the work of Christ. Pneumatology (from *pneuma* meaning 'spirit') is employed with respect to any aspect of the New Testament's understanding of the Holy Spirit. Cosmology derives from the Greek word *kosmos* which means the 'world' or 'universe', and so the cosmology of the New Testament is its understanding of the natural world. Eschatology (from *eschatos* meaning 'last' or 'final'), on the other hand, refers to all beliefs concerning the end of the world or final matters. Anthropology (from *anthropos* meaning 'man') is the term that focuses on what is believed about the nature of man, while the term ecclesiology (from *ekklesia* meaning 'assembly' or 'church') embraces all ideas relating to the church or believing community. Ethics (from *ethos* meaning 'custom' or 'usage' and *ethikos* meaning 'relating to morals') is the term used for all teaching relating to the moral behaviour which is deemed to govern the relationship between the Christian believer, the believing community and the world. Armed with these categories, then, we can now review the nature and development of Christian belief in the New Testament period.

In common with other Jews, the primitive church believed in one supreme God. In this respect, they were monotheists. This God was considered omnipresent, omnipotent and omniscient. He had created the world, he was active in nature, and he intervened in human affairs through his agents. This belief pervades the New Testament, and changed little in the course of the first Christian century.

What was distinctive about the first Christians was not their theology, which they shared with fellow Jews, but their Christology. For them, God had intervened in history, in the ministry, death and resurrection of Jesus. Jesus was seen initially by them as a prophet announcing the end-time (an eschatological prophet) or even as God's Son in the sense that he had been adopted by God to proclaim his coming kingdom. He was crucified, but, according to primitive belief, had been resurrected. His message, and his status, therefore, had been vindicated. Henceforth, he was to be seen no longer as the eschatological prophet announcing the kingdom but as the Messiah who had inaugurated it and was about to return to establish it for all time. As Christianity developed, and especially as it entered the Gentile world, where polytheism rather than monotheism was the natural or accepted form of belief, the tendency was to view Jesus less and less as a merely human figure acting on God's behalf and exalted by him, and more and more as a semi-divine, and eventually an almost fully divine figure effecting universal salvation. Here, one calls to mind Pliny's description of Asia Minor Christians reciting 'by turns a form of words to Christ as a god'.

This development in Christology is also reflected in soteriology. The primitive tradition emphasized resurrection as the vindication of God's messenger, and hence of the message. Hellenistic–Jewish or Gentile influence, especially that of Paul, placed the emphasis more on the crucifixion. Jesus had not simply inaugurated, as Messiah, the new age in which those who responded to his message would share, but had himself effected a new way to God on the cross. Access to God was by him, therefore. The Jewish law, the Temple and its cultus were therefore redundant. Christ had superseded these through his own atoning sacrifice. The trend to be discerned here, therefore, is that the 'gospel', the primitive Christian proclamation, which was initially 'good news' about the inbreaking of the Messianic age in the course of time became the 'good news' about Jesus' dying for men's sins.

In the primitive Jewish–Christian tradition, the Spirit was regarded as it was in the Old Testament or Hebrew Bible, namely, as an impersonal, external force like a wind (cf. *ruach/pneuma* = wind) that proceeded from God and enabled individuals to perform particular feats of strength, a 'power' that possessed them for a definite period, and for a definite task (cf. Judg. 15:14–17). The Jews believed in a special outpouring of this Spirit or power in the Messianic age (cf. Joel 2:28–32). Early Christians believed that Jesus was possessed by this power or Spirit (cf. Mk 1:9–13). In turn, it was believed that the primitive church had been endowed with this power. On them had been bestowed a force that enabled them to work miracles, or to perform exorcisms, like him, or that produced charismatic gifts and ecstatic states of speech (e.g. *glossolalia*). This primitive understanding of the Spirit changed or developed over time. In Luke chapter 11, verse 20 it is a sign of the new age to come. According to Paul, it is a foretaste (an 'earnest, pledge') of the new age to come (cf. 2 Cor. 1:22, 5:5). In some passages, it comes to be 'humanized', being viewed as an 'inner presence' producing moral traits rather than an 'external force' producing charismatic gifts (cf. Gal. 5:22). In other passages still, it is 'Christianized' by being identified with Jesus himself (cf. 2 Cor. 3:17–18; Acts 16:7). In John chapter 20, verse 22, for example, he breathes it, we are told, upon his disciples. In yet further passages, it is 'personalized', becoming a 'person' sent by God or Christ to the church after Jesus goes to heaven (cf. Jn 14:26, 15:26, 16:13). Eventually, in later Christian doctrine (though outside of the New Testament), it becomes the third Person of the Trinity. The trend here to be discerned in pneumatology, then, is for monotheism to develop into trinitarianism, for belief in one God to develop into belief in three (whether modes, aspects or persons).

The cosmology of the early Christians was not particularly distinctive. They shared essentially the same world view as the Jewish and Hellenistic citizens of the Roman empire, namely, a three-decker universe consisting of the earth with heaven above and hell below, and beliefs about the intervention of supernatural powers in human affairs, demons, angels, demon-possession, exorcism, miracles and so on.

What was distinctive about early Christians vis-à-vis the wider Hellenistic world, was their eschatology. Hellenism did not tend to think in terms of the end of one world, or the beginning of a new age or world (except perhaps in relation to that ushered in by the Emperor). Hellenism tended to believe in the world 'above' rather than the world 'to come', or the world 'in the future'. The world 'to come' was seen in individualistic terms, as life after death, or the immortality of the soul. There was greater emphasis, if you like, on space (verticality) than on time (horizontality). Salvation tended to be seen as the ascent of the individual to this other world, to heaven, in contrast to the Jewish view where salvation was an experience for the community, the nation, and was accompanied by the advent or arrival of the new heaven or the new earth in the future, and on the plane of history. The primitive church, or Jewish Christians, being originally an apocalyptic sect, held to the Jewish view.

When Christianity entered the wider Gentile world, however, and particularly when the expected *parousia* of Jesus did not occur, eschatology came to be de-emphasized or reinterpreted. Christianity, as a result, tended to express itself more in terms of a Graeco-Roman cosmology. Jesus the Christ became Jesus Christ, a divine being who descended from the world above. As such he could impart 'knowledge' of this world above. As such, too, he could impart 'eternal life' to the individual believer. 'Eternal life' tended to be seen no longer as the life of the age to come, the kingdom of God, a cosmic or supernatural event to be experienced by the community, but as the personal relationship of the individual believer with God or the divine Christ here and now. This emphasis can be seen, for example, in John's Gospel, the Fourth Gospel, which was written at the end of the first century CE. The trend to be discerned, therefore, may be described as a move from eschatology to Christ-mysticism.

In relation to these developments in cosmology and eschatology, one can detect a certain ambiguity in the New Testament's anthropology. The Hellenistic view of man was of an incarnate soul, while the Jewish view envisaged him as an animated body. Hellenism tended towards 'dualism', i.e. the belief that man was made up of at least two components, the body and the soul, the former often being seen as evil, the latter divine or immortal. In Hellenistic religious systems, therefore, one frequently encounters the notion that the body is a prison from which the soul must escape – the *soma* (body) *sema* (prison) view. Judaism tended towards 'monism', i.e. the belief that man was a unity created by God, that no part was capable of independent existence after death, and that if there were to be an afterlife, then the body must be reconstituted through resurrection in the context of the Messianic Age. The confusion often found in New Testament writers regarding the afterlife (cf. e.g. Paul in 2 Cor. 5:1–5) seems to stem from the overlap between these two alternative anthropological viewpoints, and it was the Hellenistic one that eventually won out in Christian thought.

Where ecclesiology is concerned, we can say that it is unlikely that the historical Jesus ever intended to found a 'church' as such. The church as an institution was a later development. Jesus instead called, or selected, a body of twelve disciples, who were perhaps representative of the twelve tribes of Israel. They were thus the symbolic or representative community of the new age. His mission, and theirs, was confined to the Jewish nation. His message, and theirs, was to announce God's coming kingdom, and to urge and exhort their fellow Jews to prepare for it. Before they went the length and breadth of Israel, the kingdom, and the Son of Man (its inaugurator), would come (cf. Mt. 10:5ff., and esp. v.23). This message was rejected by the Jews, however, and Jesus was crucified as a Messianic pretender. Nevertheless, the primitive community continued to see itself as the 'true' Israel. Like the Qumran sectarians, they awaited their Messiah, in this case the returning Jesus as the Son of Man (cf. Mt. 24:24–31). As a community they may be described, therefore, as a Jewish apocalyptic sect (or in contemporary terms, a millenarian movement), and indeed, given the reaction of their fellow Jews to their eschatological message, as a *despised* and *persecuted* apocalyptic sect.

Although rejected by the Jews, a form of the early Christian proclamation, as we have seen, was accepted by Gentiles, somewhat against the primitive church's expectation. In Gentile Christianity, or even in Hellenistic–Jewish Christianity, Christ was seen as having superceded the old law, the old covenant, the Temple. The emergent Christian community was now a body largely of Gentile Christians, with Jewish Christians in the minority, who saw themselves as the 'new' Israel (cf. Gal. 6:15–16). In union with Christ, Christian believers, Paul claims, are God's 'new Temple', for God's Spirit dwells in them (cf. 1 Cor. 3:16–17; Jn 2:18–22). The 'church' was viewed as the body of Christ, a body of Spirit-filled believers.

This conception is found in Paul, but by the time of the Pastoral Epistles (attributed to Paul but by a later hand) at the end of the century a different conception from this dynamic one has developed. Here, the church is an established institution with its own creed, body of inspired scripture or canon, and offices and office-bearers, even a primitive episcopate. This church describes itself as a 'pillar and bulwark of truth' (1 Tim. 3:15). It has a tradition to defend, and to pass on to other generations. It is aware of its past, and looks to an ongoing future. Its function is to 'guard the deposit', in other words, the tradition it has received from the apostles. It has come to terms with the Gentile world and its concern is to maintain a respectable place in it. Its injunctions to believers are prompted by the desire that the church be not brought into disrepute. Eschatology has been all but eclipsed. The Spirit takes a back seat. Order, organization and propriety are the key emphases. From a poor, despised, Jewish apocalyptic sect, at the beginning of the New Testament period, then, the church has all but become a respectable, bourgeois, Gentile institution at the end.

This trend is reflected also in the ethics of the New Testament. In the Pliny–Trajan correspondence we noted the apparent emphasis on the Decalogue or Ten Commandments ('took an oath not to commit theft', etc.). The ethics of the primitive community have been described as an interim ethic, i.e. its ethical injunctions were not absolute, timeless, moral prescriptions for all generations to come. The primitive community in reality recognized only two generations: this present, wicked generation under Satan's power, and the generation about to participate in the new age. Its moral injunctions were originally, then, 'councils of prudence', short-term, relative, urgent and expedient responses to the exciting and breathtaking situation that faced them, namely, the advent of the kingdom of God. Their attitude to wealth provides an apt example. Jesus and his first disciples exhorted their fellow Jews to sell all that they had and to follow them. This was not because poverty was a way of life to be followed henceforth as a good in itself. This was the attitude of the later church. Poverty was espoused because riches and possessions gave one a stake in the present age, and so were unnecessary since this age was about to pass away. It was better to abandon them in light of the coming day of the Lord. The passage in Acts chapter 2, verses 43–47 is also instructive. The primitive church, Luke tells us, held all things in common. They practised a form of communism, or better, of communalism. This was not because they were primitive Marxists. To see them as such ignores the eschatological dimension in which primitive Christianity was conceived. They did so, not because they regarded this as a better economic system, or as a challenge to the present economic order in favour of a better one, but because as a community they were preparing themselves, holding themselves in readiness for the close of history, the supernatural intervention of God in the form of his Messiah Jesus, the start of a new age. Their common meals are to be seen in this light too. This brings us to the practice of the early church, to which we now turn.

As with Christian belief, I have included a table (Table 3, overleaf) giving a number of the key technical terms used with respect to Christian practice, and this too can be consulted for the definitions involved. Let us begin with Christian worship.

In enquiring after the worship of the early church, we might ask what a typical church meeting was like in New Testament

Table 3 The early church (practice)

Term	Meaning	From Greek (or Latin)
Sacrament	Rite or ritual in which a deity is made 'present' to the believer or by which the believer is 'bound' to or 'united' with the deity (cf. e.g. the Christian Eucharist or Baptism)	*sacramentum* = oath (Latin); that by which a person solemnly binds himself or another to anything
Baptism	A rite using water as a symbol of religious purification	*baptizo* = to dip, immerse in water
Eucharist	The Christian sacrament of the Lord's Supper	*eucharistein* = to give thanks
Liturgy	An act of worship which offers service to God, and especially the Eucharist	*laos* = people *ergon* = work, service
Agape	The early Christian common meal (or 'love-feast') for fellowship and charity; to be distinguished from the Eucharist	*agape* = love
Kerygma	The preaching or central proclamation of the early Church/New Testament	*kerygma* = proclamation *kerux* = herald
Didache	The teaching of the early Church/New Testament	*didache* = teaching or ethical instruction
Catechesis	Specific teaching to new members (catechumens) of the Christian community	*katecheo* = to give instruction (to initiates or 'neophytes')
Parenesis	Used of NT writings (or parts thereof) whose function was to give exhortation, advice, instruction, encouragement	*paraineo* = to urge, exhort
Apologetic	Used of NT writings (or parts thereof) whose function was to give a defence of the point of view represented	*apologia* = an argument in defence or vindication of a person, cause, etc.
Polemic	Used of NT writings (or parts thereof) whose function was to make an attack on opponents or points of view being resisted	*polemeo* = to attack

times. This appears a simple question, but it needs some qualification in light of the diversity apparent in the New Testament. The New Testament witnesses to different forms of Christianity in the early period. One may talk of Jewish Christianity, Hellenistic–Jewish Christianity or Gentile Christianity. One may also speak of Apocalyptic Christianity, of Pauline Christianity, of Johannine Christianity or that Christianity which began to appear at the end of the first century and early second century, emergent Catholicism. The New Testament writings and the traditions they embody derive from different Christian communities and from different periods in early church history. The Pliny–Trajan correspondence gave an outsider's view of the worship of the Christian community in Asia Minor (Bithynia) at the beginning of the second century CE. For the insider's view, we may equally take note of Luke's idealized picture of the primitive Jewish–Christian community's worship in Jerusalem (cf. Acts 2:42, 46, 5:42). In the letters of Paul, and especially in 1 Corinthians chapter 11, verses 20ff. and chapter 14, we can see what worship was like for a Pauline community in Greece. In the book of Revelation, on the other hand, we have a mine of information on the nature of Christian worship in Asia Minor in the reign of Emperor Domitian (81–96 CE).

Despite this diversity, however, some general questions and answers are possible. When and where did Christians tend to meet? What were the basic components of their worship? What developments took place in the New Testament period?

In asking when, we must bear in mind that the primitive Christian community was Jewish, and hence their 'Sunday' was the sabbath, the last day of the week, according to Gentiles, today's 'Saturday'. They met daily, according to early writers like Luke, in view of the imminence of Christ's *parousia* (cf. Acts 2:46, 5:42). In the Pauline churches, they met weekly, on the first day of the week, a practice that may reflect the waning of eschatological expectancy (cf. 1 Cor. 16:2). The first day of the week commemorated Christ's resurrection. It came to be known, therefore, as the 'Lord's day' (cf. Rev. 1:9, 10). Much later (in the fourth century CE) this day became today's 'Sunday' when the symbolism of the heathen sun cult (Mithras) was appropriated by Christians as a symbol of the resurrection. Up until then it was a normal working day, with two brief periods of worship, before dawn and in the evening (compare again the Pliny-Trajan correspondence). Only in Emperor Constantine's reign (306–337 CE) did it become a holiday, with Jewish Sabbath regulations being subsequently attached to it.

Where did early Christians meet for worship? Since the primitive Christian community were Jews, they worshipped in the Temple (cf. Acts 5:42), or in the synagogue, as Jesus had done (cf. Lk. 4:16). Later in the century, in consequence of the Council of Jamnia (c. 90 CE), Jewish Christians were expelled from the synagogue. Many of the features of early Christian worship and practice, nevertheless, were taken over from the synagogue. Early Christians also met in each other's homes (cf. Acts 2:46, 5:42; 1 Cor. 16:19; Rom. 16:5).

What was the nature of early Christian worship, and what were the meetings like? The expectation that Jesus would return, the belief in the imminent end of the world in the primitive Jewish–Christian community (the *Urgemeinde*), and the conviction in the Pauline communities that Christ was already present to some extent through his Spirit meant that for those early Christian communities worship was conducted in an atmosphere of intense excitement or excitability. Forms of worship in this period, therefore, especially in the Pauline churches, were relatively unstructured, fluid, spontaneous, dynamic and charismatic (cf. 1 Cor. 11–14).

Two phenomena are here worthy of note, namely *glossolalia* and prophecy. To the insider, *glossolalia* or 'speaking in tongues' is an inspired, ecstatic, but unintelligible form of speech in which the believer communes on a different wavelength with his God. To the outsider, it is hysterical raving. *Glossolalia* was a particular feature of the Pauline churches (cf. 1 Cor. 14) but it died out in the later New Testament period.

A second phenomenon was that of prophecy. The prophets were a very prominent group in the early church (cf. Acts 11:28, 13:1–3 and the Revelation of John, *passim*). They were deemed to have gifts of clairvoyance, and of inspired, ecstatic utterance. Unlike *glossolalia*, their inspired utterances were intelligible, and were designed to edify, not the individual believer, but the community as a whole. Christian prophets were deemed to possess the Spirit *par excellence*. Christ himself was believed to speak through them to the church. They were his mediums. The prophets were as esteemed as the apostles in the early generations, before their highly individualistic and charismatic style became a threat to established ecclesiastical law and order. In the end, these 'prophets' of the New Testament were eclipsed by the new 'priests' of the developing church, the permanent officials, bishops, elders, deacons, the new hierarchy. What the New Testament owes to them is perhaps, among other things, certain sayings which are found on Jesus' lips (e.g. Rev. 1:17–18, 3:20, 16:15), and various snatches of hymns, prayers, benedictions, doxologies, and exhortations which are embedded like nuggets in our texts. Others, of course, have been taken over from Judaism. As time went on, then, forms of worship, originally relatively spontaneous, became more formal and formalized. As Pliny observed, these early Christians by the time of the early second century CE were accustomed 'to recite by turns a form of words [*carmen dicere*] to Christ as a god'.

One feature of early Christian worship is the development of what have come to be called the sacraments. The Latin word *sacramentum* from which the expression derives literally means an 'oath' (and was used, one recalls, by Pliny when he referred to early Christians binding themselves 'with an oath'). The word has now come to mean a rite or ritual binding a believer to his God. Two major sacraments are associated with the early church, namely, baptism and the eucharist. The origins of the first, baptism, are disputed. Jesus, according to John chapter 4, verse 2, did not himself baptize, it appears. Whence this rite, then, so important, and so distinctive, for early Christianity? Various antecedents have been suggested. Some look to the mystery religions (described in chapter 1) who practiced esoteric initiation rites in which the believer united with his or her god through immersion. The practice, it is claimed, was taken over by Christianity when it spread into the wider Hellenistic world. Influences closer to home and earlier, however, have also been posited, such as Jewish proselyte baptism or the Qumran community. In the former, when Gentiles (proselytes) converted to Judaism, circumcision was preceded by ceremonial purification from pollution, and some scholars speculate that Jewish Christians likewise insisted upon this rite of immersion for Gentiles entering the community of the 'true Israel'. The Essenes also practised a form of ritual lustration (although this was regular and purificatory, rather than initiatory) and so the rite may have entered primitive Christianity in consequence of early links between the Christian movement and the Qumran community. The weight of evidence, however, would seem to support those who claim that Christian baptismal practice was taken over from the sect founded by John the Baptist, with whom Jesus himself had close links. John insisted that all Jews be baptized, it seems, the nation being as corrupt in his view as Gentiles, and in need, therefore, of moral cleansing.

Christian baptism distinguished itself from that of the Baptist sect by virtue of its association with the conferring of the Spirit (cf. Mk 1:9–11; Acts 2:38, 19:1ff.). John's baptism was for repentance from sins, while Christian baptism promised more than ritual forgiveness. It promised the Spirit (although the pattern 'baptism then Spirit' is not always uniform in the book of Acts; cf. e.g. Acts 10:47–48). What is clear from the New Testament is that the original significance of the rite was eschatological. The initiate was baptized into the eschatological community (the community of the new age), and as a sign that the new age was dawning, the Spirit was conferred on him (or her).

Certain developments can be traced, however, in the meaning given to this important rite. In the Pauline letters, echoing the mystery religions, baptism is viewed as a symbol for dying and rising with Christ (cf. Rom. 6), an act in which the believer is united with Christ in his death and resurrection. The act came, it appears, to be regarded in a semi-magical way, namely as a means of securing salvation here and now, through union with Christ (cf. 1 Pet. 3:21). As time went on, it became more formalized, with baptismal instruction being extended to the Christian initiate (cf. 1 Pet. 1:3–4:6 which may reflect an early baptismal liturgy) in a baptismal service which was later limited to the Easter season. Originally, baptism was by total immersion (in 'running water', according to the Didache) but as time went on other means (e.g. sprinkling) became normative, and, in some quarters, the rite was deemed capable of being extended to children.

The second major sacrament is the eucharist (or the Lord's supper, or communion, as it is known in different ecclesiastical or denominational circles). Here, too, the origin of the rite is disputed, some again claiming the influence of the mystery religions (and their sacred meals) on early Christianity, others suggesting that it is rooted in the fellowship meals held in Jewish circles, particularly that of the Passover. It is in this latter context that the Gospels present it. The eucharist or Lord's supper as a modern Christian recognizes it has little connection, however, with that held in the New Testament period. The modern eucharist is the product of a long process of theological reflection and ecclesiastical development and practice.

As far as we can determine, the original eucharistic meal was a common fellowship meal whose import again seems to have been eschatological. It seems to have been a joyful occasion (*eucharistein* means 'to give thanks') when the primitive Jewish-Christian community, which shared all things in common, met together to eat a common meal. As they met, they looked to the imminent future in which Jesus would return shortly as Messiah;

in which they, as the 'true Israel', would participate in the new age; in which they themselves would share in the Messianic banquet, a promised feature of that age. As they met, they also looked to the recent past when they had often shared such meals with Jesus (especially perhaps his last meal with them before his death) and at which he had reminded them of the age to come. In the Pauline communities, that sense of Jesus' presence was particularly reinforced through the belief in the 'Spirit' and emphasized through prophecy.

A number of developments took place in this original common meal, both theologically and sociologically. Theologically, the emphasis shifted from an eschatological to a soteriological one. The primitive eschatological emphasis viewed the common meal, as we have stated, as an anticipation of the new age, especially the Messianic banquet. It also celebrated Jesus' resurrection as a vindication of his eschatological message and status. In Pauline Christianity, the emphasis shifted to the cross, and this emphasis is reflected in eucharistic doctrine. Reflection on the last meal Jesus had had with his disciples, and especially its Passover setting, led to the view that his death had in itself an atoning significance, i.e. it was seen as a sacrifice. The Fourth Gospel takes this a step further. Where the Synoptic Gospels (Matthew, Mark and Luke) have Jesus and his disciples eat what is undoubtedly a Passover meal, and then describe Jesus as having been crucified after Passover, the Fourth Gospel has Jesus crucified immediately before the Passover proper, at the very time the Passover lambs are being sacrificed in the Temple. The soteriological implications of this have not been lost on numerous commentators. The difference of dating between the Synoptic Gospels and that of John was appealed to in later times by the Roman church and the churches in Asia Minor who celebrated Easter at different times: the Roman church celebrated it on the first Friday (–Sunday) after the Jewish Passover, the latter on the Jewish Passover itself, whatever day it fell.

From a sociological perspective, changes in this original common meal were equally striking. The first 'eucharists' were actually full-scale fellowship meals, usually held in the evenings and in the homes of early Christians (compare again the Pliny–Trajan correspondence). The meal was called an *agape* or 'love-feast'. The sacrament we know as the Lord's supper or eucharist developed within these love-feasts, but eventually became detached from them, developing along its own ritual lines, until it became in the end a solemn rite administered in a church setting by a church official to believers. The impetus for this development came, among other things, from the abuses to which these love-feasts became subject (for an early example, see Acts 6:1–6; 1 Cor. 11:17–34). From their idealistic first days, these common love-feasts quickly degenerated and became occasions for class distinctions to be paraded, for envy, for gluttony or for drunkenness. Having become charity meals, they were finally prohibited by church decree in the seventh century CE.

We come finally to church order and organization, as it is reflected in the writings of the New Testament. As mentioned above, it is now generally agreed that Jesus did not intend to found a church in our sense of the word, an institution, that is, with definite functions or offices, and far less that these offices should reflect a visible hierarchy. The church as such is a later development. The only passages in the New Testament even approximating to such a claim are from the Gospel of Matthew (16:17–20, 18:15–20) and here they are, by common consent, an addition by Matthew to his source, Mark, reflecting a later attitude or development which has been retrojected onto Jesus' lips (the term *ekklesia* meaning the 'church' is found nowhere else in the Gospels). What the historical Jesus did was to gather a group of disciples and send them out to proclaim to their fellow Jews that God's kingdom was about to come. The selection of the twelve, if historical, might reflect his intention that they be seen as the symbolic representatives of the twelve tribes of Israel (cf. Mt.19:28 and Lk.22:30). The eschatological environment in which primitive Christianity was conceived precludes any thought of the church being founded by Jesus as an institution to transmit his teaching from generation to generation. What we see, therefore, with the waning of eschatological expectation, is a gradual transition from the idea of the 'church' as a community of Jews called to proclaim to their fellow Jews the imminent end of the world, to the church as a universal institution founded to transform that world. This trend can be detected to some degree in the New Testament writings from the early to the late period, although it is after the New Testament period itself that the church, in anything like our sense of the word definitely emerges.

This can be briefly illustrated by reference to the varying leadership patterns discernible in the New Testament period. In Jewish Christianity, as we have seen, the leadership of the primitive community was in the hands of Jesus' family, in particular his brother James, and then his cousin Simeon. In the Pauline churches of the Diaspora, by contrast, organization and leadership was extremely fluid, and tended to be based, not on traditional authority, but on what sociologists term 'charismatic' authority. We hear, therefore, of apostles, prophets, teachers, administrators, those with gifts of miracle-working, healing, speaking in tongues, etc. (cf. 1 Cor. 12:28).

The Acts of the Apostles also conveys an impression of no fixed order or organization. Mention is made of a leadership role over the Hellenistic wing of primitive Christianity by the 'seven' appointed by the Jerusalem apostles, but little is made of this. Reference is also made to the appointment by Paul of 'elders' (curiously not mentioned in the genuine Pauline letters) but these may be equivalent to the 'overseers' (*episkopoi*) mentioned in, for example, Paul's letter to the Philippians (1:1) in that they share the same function, namely pastoral care, oversight and teaching (cf. Acts 14:23, 20:17–38).

It is in the Pastoral Epistles, at the turn of the century, that reference to more fixed offices is found: deacons, elders and *the* 'bishop' (again *episkopos*). There is clearly ambiguity over the significance of this word. It can mean 'elder' but since it is used only in the singular, it may connote someone who was either *primus inter pares*, that is equal to the other elders, but exercising a special duty of oversight, or who might even represent the monarchical bishop who was to emerge as one of the major officials of second-century Christianity. It is only in the Letters of Ignatius in the early second century CE that we find definite evidence for the emergence of an established monarchical episcopacy. The Pastoral Epistles may, therefore, represent a step on the way to this institution, since they do not describe the nature of these offices (deacons, elders, the e*piskopos*) but only the qualifications required of candidates for them. Such individuals were ordained, however, by the laying on of hands, a procedure borrowed from Judaism, but signifying that apostolic authority had been deemed to have passed to them.

Let me sum up this rather complicated discussion. In the second half of this chapter, I have focused on the nature and development of early Christian belief and practice. I noted certain trends within the New Testament period and certain shifts in emphasis in respect of a number of major areas of Christian belief by the end of that period. I summarized these beliefs in respect of the major areas of theology, Christology, soteriology, pneumatology, cosmology, anthropology, eschatology, ecclesiology and ethics.

Where belief about God (theology) was concerned, I noted the shift from monotheism in Jewish Christianity towards trinitarianism in the emergent Catholic church. From belief in one God, we see a move towards belief in one God with three aspects, modes, faces or persons.

Where belief about the person of Jesus (Christology) was concerned, the gradual divinization of Jesus is a matter for comment. Starting from a 'low' Christology, the New Testament writings witness to an ever greater 'high' Christology (or perhaps, as in the case of Paul, from a relatively 'high' Christology to a yet higher one). In the beginning, Jesus is seen as a human figure acting on God's behalf, as an individual adopted by God (and hence his 'son' in this sense) to proclaim his coming kingdom. By the end of the New Testament period, Jesus has come to be viewed as a semi-divine, in some cases fully-divine figure, sharing God's own nature. This progression is captured very well in the title of a recent book by M. Casey, *From Jewish Prophet to Gentile God* (1991).[31] Jesus, the Jewish prophet, the one believed to be Messiah by his first followers, becomes Jesus, the Son of God, an incarnation of God himself.

Where the work of this Jesus is concerned (soteriology), from salvation viewed as participation in the new age proclaimed by Jesus, and about to be ushered in by him as returning Messiah, we see the belief developing that access to God has been effected through Jesus' atoning sacrifice on the cross. 'Good news' as 'good news' (gospel) about the inbreaking of the Messianic Age becomes 'good news' or 'gospel' about Jesus' dying for humankind's sins.

A further aspect of early Christian belief concerns the Spirit (pneumatology). From the Spirit as an external force or power behind charismatic gifts that are seen as a sign of the in-breaking of the new age, we encounter the Spirit as an inner, moral presence, the third Person of the Trinity, given to the church as its permanent possession, as comforter and guide.

Similar changes attend early Christian belief about the world (cosmology), its demise (eschatology) and the nature of man (anthropology). From the belief that the old world is about to pass away and a new world about to come in the imminent future, we see the development of belief in a parallel 'world above', here and now, to which the individual can have access through Christ. Eschatology is gradually eclipsed and a Christ-mysticism takes its place. Eclipsing resurrection as a reconstitution in the new age of the unified body created by God is the notion of the immortality of the soul, and its escape into the afterlife from the trammels of the body.

Where the understanding of the church is concerned (ecclesiology), we begin with a despised Jewish apocalyptic sect and end with a respectable (even bourgeois) Gentile institution. And in the matter of relations between believers and the world (ethics), ethical injunctions which begin as short-term, interim, urgent, expedient responses to the imminent dissolution of the established world-order, end as absolute, moral prescriptions for all generations.

So much for belief. Similar developments can be charted for practice. Forms of worship which were in the beginning spontaneous tend to become more formalized at the end of the New Testament period. The sacraments undergo shifts in emphasis. From baptism seen as entry into the eschatological community, the community of the new age, we see baptism becoming a rite symbolizing entry into the universal church (and perhaps securing salvation as a result). From the common meal seen as a joyful anticipation of the Messianic banquet in the new age, the eucharist becomes a solemn rite which unites believers with the God-Man whose atoning sacrifice has secured their forgiveness.

Ecclesiastical organization also undergoes similar shifts. From a group of Jews called to proclaim to their fellow Jews the imminent end of the world, we end up with a universal institution of Gentiles with its own creed, canon of scripture and episcopacy founded to transform that world. These developments in the belief, worship and organization of the early Church are all reflected in the literature produced by the Church, and it is to this literature, the New Testament, that we are now ready to turn.

3

The New Testament

The emergence of the New Testament

In our last chapter, we examined the origins and history of the early church, and the nature and development of early Christian belief and practice. One aspect of early Christian belief and practice was the value attached to and the use made of holy scripture. The Bible of the primitive church was the Hebrew Bible, what Christians call the 'Old Testament'. Unlike their fellow Jews, early Christians interpreted it differently. They focused on passages which allowed for an eschatological or Messianic interpretation. Because they believed Jesus was the Messiah, they interpreted it in this light. It was the source-book for their Christology. It spoke to them of Christ. He was reflected in its pages. He had fulfilled the prophecies contained in it.

The Hebrew Bible was read out, therefore, as part of their services, as in the synagogue. Books were costly, people were illiterate, and hence this was the only way of getting to know the scriptures. Was there a set order of reading? We don't know, but the Jewish synagogue (we are not entirely sure when) developed the practice of planning the reading of the law within either a one-year (Babylonia) or three-year cycle (Palestine), and appropriate readings were also devised for festivals. Did Christians follow this practice too? There are those who answer in the affirmative, and some who even theorize that the literary structure of the Gospels reveals that they were originally composed for liturgical reading.

What passages were selected? Here we are on firmer ground, as by virtue of its eschatological and apocalyptic concerns, the early church made frequent use of certain passages and books (e.g. the Psalms, the Major and Minor Prophets, apocalyptic writings like the book of Daniel) at the expense of others.[32] Other writings were also read out (e.g. Paul's letters, the Gospels, the Revelation of John). Such readings were then followed by

---

The New Testament writings

The Gospel according to Matthew
The Gospel according to Mark
The Gospel according to Luke
The Gospel according to John
The Acts of the Apostles
The Letter of Paul to the Romans
The First Letter of Paul to the Corinthians
The Second Letter of Paul to the Corinthians
The Letter of Paul to the Galatians
The Letter of Paul to the Ephesians
The Letter of Paul to the Philippians
The Letter of Paul to the Colossians
The First Letter of Paul to the Thessalonians
The Second Letter of Paul to the Thessalonians
The First Letter of Paul to Timothy
The Second Letter of Paul to Timothy
The Letter of Paul to Titus
The Letter of Paul to Philemon
The Epistle to the Hebrews
The Letter of James
The First Letter of Peter
The Second Letter of Peter
The First Letter of John
The Second Letter of John
The Third Letter of John
The Letter of Jude
The Revelation of John

---

preaching, teaching and exhortation. Eventually these other writings were regarded as a second body of scripture witnessing to the 'new covenant' God had made with his new Israel, the church, i.e. the New Testament. Thus (but over a period of three centuries) the New Testament canon emerged.

Just what is the nature of the New Testament? Five observations can be made. In the first place, one may say that the New Testament, viewed from a historical perspective, is *not a book but a collection of writings*. They are listed, some twenty-seven in number, in the box on the previous page. These writings are in Greek, although the Greek style is not uniform. Sometimes it is almost classical, as in the Gospel of Luke. At other times it is vulgar, ungrammatical and highly Semitic, as in the Revelation of John. With the exception of the genuine Pauline letters, these writings were mostly produced after 70 CE, unless one accepts the controversial dating of J. A. T. Robinson in *Redating the New Testament*.[33] They represent a variety of different literary forms or genres, e.g. gospels, epistles or letters,[34] a theological history of early Christianity (the Acts of the Apostles) and an apocalypse (the Revelation of John).

Second, these writings embody *not the early Christian tradition but only a selection of the available traditions* of Christian communities in the Mediterranean world between 30 and 150 CE. This selection is, moreover, incomplete, and in a number of ways problematic for the historian. The writings are not placed in any chronological order. The dating is difficult. The selection is unbalanced. Of the twenty-seven that have come down to us, thirteen, i.e. almost half, are attributed to the apostle Paul, or to adherents of Gentile or Pauline Christianity. Other traditions have not survived, or survive only in an emaciated form, for example, the conjectural sayings source, Q, of primitive Jewish Christianity, which scholars believe has been independently incorporated into the Gospels of Matthew and Luke.

Third, the New Testament reflects *not one religious viewpoint but many*. In his letter to the Galatians, for example, the apostle Paul places great emphasis on the notion of what has been called 'justification by faith', as opposed to justification by works (Gal. 2:15–16).[35] This view, on the other hand, is criticized in the Letter of James (cf. Jas 2:18–26), a difference in theological emphasis which explains why the reformer, Martin Luther, dismissed the latter as 'an epistle of straw'.

Fourth, as we have already noted, the New Testament presents *not one kerygma but a variety of different proclamations or kerygmata*. All the New Testament writings are united in their witness to the significance of Jesus, but when they come to express that witness, they offer a variety of interpretations of the significance of his teaching and activity, of his life and death. And this is not surprising, since these writings have emanated from different Christian communities of the Mediterranean world at different times and under different circumstances. The New Testament as a result presents us not with the history surrounding Jesus' life and death, but with various theological interpretations of that history.

This interpretation took various forms, and was embodied in various traditions. These traditions were in turn interpreted and reinterpreted. The various proclamations of Christian faith or *kerygmata*, were conceived in or adapted to their respective environments. We should distinguish, therefore, between the proclamation of the primitive church in Palestine, that of Hellenistic–Jewish Christians to their fellow Jews in the Diaspora, and that in turn by missionaries in and to the Gentile world. There is the proclamation, too, of the post-apostolic Gentile churches after 70 CE. Indeed, it is in this last environment that the majority of the New Testament writings were conceived. It would not be an exaggeration to claim, therefore, that there are almost as many variations in the *kerygma* as there are New Testament writers.[36] Even in Paul, we can discern variations between the earliest and the latest of his proclamations.

Our final observation follows from, and sums up, the rest and it is that the New Testament represents *not one form of early Christianity but various forms of early Christianity*. Hence, it is inaccurate to speak of early Christianity as if it were one entity. The New Testament witnesses to various forms of early Christianity with different, often contrasting or even incompatible emphases or viewpoints. So, for example, we encounter in its pages apocalyptic Christianity, whose world-view is discernible in the earliest strata of the Gospels of Mark and Matthew, in the sayings source Q, or in the last book of the New Testament, the Revelation of John. We can observe Pauline Christianity as it finds expression in the Pauline letters and the Deutero-Pauline (or secondary) literature influenced by him. We can speak of a contrasting Johannine Christianity as it appears in the Fourth Gospel and the Johannine Epistles. And we can recognize the distinctive features of early or emergent Catholicism as they reveal themselves to us in the so-called Catholic Epistles of 1 and 2 Peter, James or Jude, or in the so-called (Deutero-Pauline) Pastoral Epistles of 1 and 2 Timothy and Titus.

I have commented on the nature of the New Testament. What about its origins? The New Testament writings were relatively slow in emerging. The majority, as we have said, were written after 70 CE, hence some forty years after the death of Jesus. What were the factors inhibiting the production of a Christian literary tradition before this, and what encouraged that tradition thereafter?

Two of the factors inhibiting the initial formation of the New Testament writings were clearly economic and cultural. The cost of writing materials in the ancient world was often prohibitive, especially for the poor, and the first Christians were, for the most part, poor, uneducated and illiterate (cf. 1 Cor. l:26ff. 'not many of you were wise . . . influential . . . of noble birth'). Jewish

Christians in Palestine, in particular, may have been accustomed to indigence or destitution. The name adopted by one of the second-century Jewish–Christian sects which laid claim to a descent from the Jerusalem church or *Urgemeinde* was the Ebionites, which means 'the poor ones'.[37] Books were written on papyrus (parchment), or on animal skins (vellum), and hence were expensive. Most people had to make do with broken pieces of pottery (*ostraca*) or wood for record-keeping or brief communications.

Religious factors have also to be taken into consideration. In the first place, Jesus himself never wrote anything (New Testament scholarship would surely be very different if he had!). This is not surprising, however, given his role as an eschatological messenger or proclaimer of God's coming kingdom, a prophet announcing the end of the present age and the advent of the new.

In the second place, this proclamation was taken over by the primitive church who saw Jesus in turn as the Messiah about to return in the imminent future. In light of this belief, their concerns were intensely practical, therefore, rather than literary. These concerns were to preach, urge, warn, and summon their fellow Jews to repentance, and to edify, encourage, and exhort their fellow Christians to faithfulness. Both activities were largely by word of mouth. Both were conducted in light of Jesus' coming *parousia*.

Third, the primitive church already had a Bible, as we have seen, a body of inspired scripture, namely the Old Testament (or Hebrew Bible). Its proclamation was founded on the claim that Jesus had fulfilled Old Testament prophecies concerning Messiahship and the Messianic Age. There is some reason to suppose, therefore, that the authoritative nature of these writings for the primitive church may have had an inhibiting effect on the production of fresh books.

Fourth, Jesus was believed (particularly in Pauline communities) to be 'alive', to be present already through his Spirit, especially through prophecy and the prophets. What need for written traditions about him if his living voice addressed them through the Christian prophets?

In the fifth place, the primitive church was composed of Jews for whom the oral tradition was extremely important and valued. It took centuries, one recalls, for rabbis to commit to writing the oral tradition that had developed in relation to the Torah, that is the Mishnah, c.200 CE. In the 'tunnel' period, the primitive community had Jesus' original disciples and their living procla-mation. In this same period, the primitive community had the first believers and their witness. Even after 70 CE, the preference for oral tradition continued to be expressed, as, for example, by the early second century Church father, Papias, who is on record as having stated:

> For I supposed that things out of books did not profit me so much as the utterances of a voice which liveth or abideth.[38]

These and other such factors may explain the initial reluctance of Christians to commit their traditions to writing. But what accounts for the subsequent formation of the New Testament writings, and their development into a distinct corpus? The first major factor must surely have been the delay (or non-arrival) of the *parousia*. As the expectation that the world was about to end waned, a gradual acceptance developed among early Christians of the world as destined to continue through the foreseeable future. This had three main effects: it compelled a fresh study or interpretation of Jesus' teaching and message; it prompted a new understanding of the nature and significance of the Christian movement; and it removed the inhibition from writing. The church was seen as an ongoing institution with a role not to proclaim the end of the world but to play its part within that world to transform it. Eschatology was giving way to salvation history, and one important result was the writing of the first church history by 'Luke' (the Acts of the Apostles). This 'history' looks back to the Old Testament and the prophets, views the time of Jesus as a sacred time, has a place for the church in the divine scheme of things, and relegates the *parousia* to a more distant future.

A second major factor was the death of the first apostles and 'eye-witnesses' of the primitive movement. With the death of the apostles, and the first generation of believers, there was a 'drying up', then, of the oral tradition, and this led to the necessity for a substitute. The need arose to produce something in concrete or written form for posterity. There was a desire that the apostolic tradition or the witness of the first disciples be preserved for coming generations. There was a desire for authority.

The third major factor was the spread of Christianity into the wider Hellenistic world. This, too, had certain important effects. In the first place, it produced the break with Judaism, the 'parting of the ways'. Christianity was no longer as close as it had been to Judaism. Oral tradition, valued in Jewish circles, was less valued in Gentile ones. The Hebrew Bible or Old Testament was less authoritative for Gentiles or Gentile–Christian communities. In the Gentile world and among Gentile–Christian communities, with the de-emphasis of eschatology, there tended to arise a stronger 'biographical' or 'historical' interest in Jesus himself, in his teaching and activity, in his words and deeds. Among Gentile–Christian, Greek-speaking communities, an impetus developed for the gathering of traditions about Jesus, especially those that presented him as superior to the divine men, philosophers, miracle-workers, heroes, gods and saviours of the Hellenistic world. If Jesus was the 'Saviour of the world', it was necessary for the sake of converts to produce something about his person as well as his message. Such factors, then, led to the formation of the Gospels.

Allied with these factors, however, was the Gentile interest in Paul, and his growing rehabilitation. In the 'tunnel' period,

Paul had been the self-appointed apostle to the Gentiles, championing their cause with an authority not derived from the historical Jesus or the Jerusalem church. Towards the end of the century, the pastoral or missionary letters to the Gentile–Christian communities he had established in Asia Minor and Europe were collected together (as many as could be found). The impetus towards a collection of Paul's letters was perhaps stimulated by the publication of Acts (which incidentally makes no reference to those letters nor seems to derive its data from them) in the latter part of the first century CE. By the middle of the second century CE, however, we have clear evidence, in 2 Peter chapter 3, verse 15, of the existence of a Pauline corpus (though not of its components).

A brief introduction to the New Testament writings

From what has been said to date, it can be seen that the New Testament writings and their component parts arose as a specific response to the needs of the various Christian communities that produced them. In other words, it was the *function* they performed in these various Christian communities that led first of all to their emergence, and then later to their accepted status (albeit variously disputed) as holy scripture, a *New* Testament as opposed to the *Old* Testament. In this section, before offering a brief introduction to the New Testament writings themselves, I want to look at the needs, functions or activities of early Christian communities which led to the emergence of the New Testament writings and the traditional material they contain. These needs, functions or activities can be described, first, in terms of what early Christian communities did, or needed to do, to maintain themselves (their *internal* needs or activities), and, second, they can be viewed from the point of view of the communities' posture towards the outside world (their *external* needs or activities). Since I shall be introducing you to a number of further technical terms, you might like to consult again the glossary given in Table 3, p. 62.

The first internal need or activity of early Christian communities was that of worship, or *leitourgia*, a Greek word meaning 'public service' ('work of/for the people'), from which we get our word 'liturgy' (a service to God). The early Christians worshipped together. Hence instruction on the sacraments, for instance, needed to be formulated and handed down. A good example, already touched upon, is the passage 1 Peter 1:3–4:6 which a number of scholars believe is a baptismal liturgy shorn of its rubrics (or practical instructions to the officiating priest) and despatched to churches in the form of a letter or epistle. Another set of passages is 1 Corinthians chapters 11 and 14 where Paul gives instructions for the conduct of church meetings in general, and for the love-feast (*agape*) and the eucharist in particular (cf. 1 Cor. 11:17–34, esp. 23–26).

A second internal need or activity was that of *parenesis*. The word comes from the Greek *paraineo* meaning to 'teach, instruct, exhort or encourage'. Parenesis refers to material in the New Testament writings which is didactic or exhortative, and it takes a variety of forms.

The first is *didache* which means 'teaching', and is from the Greek word *didaskein* meaning 'to teach'. One of the very first activities of early Christian communities was to make collections of Jesus' teachings. The supreme example is the hypothetical 'sayings' source, Q, already referred to, which Matthew and Luke, it is believed, independently incorporated into their Gospels.

The second is *catechesis* or specific instruction to catechumens, neophytes or newly baptized or about to be baptized members of the church. The word derives from the Greek verb *katecheo* meaning to 'give instruction'. Catechesis is a special form of teaching or *didache*. Parts of the Pauline letters contain catechesis, as well as *didache*, as do the Gospels. Indeed, we possess an entire early Christian writing entitled the *Didache*. This is a document, dating to the late first century CE, or early second century CE, which not only offers early Christian teaching, but gives directives for catechetical instruction, worship and ministry.

A third category is *ethical parenesis*, that is, exhortation to correct moral conduct. Such parenesis is found again in parts of the Pauline letters, and is one of Paul's reasons for writing to his converts. The genuine Pauline letters all have a specific section of ethical parenesis (cf. e.g. Rom. 12ff.; Gal. 5:1ff.; 1 Thess. 4:1ff.). Some of these sections incorporate Jewish or Hellenistic ethical codes, in particular catalogues of virtues (cf. e.g. Phil. 4:8: 'Finally, brethren, whatever is true, whatever is honourable, whatever is just, whatever is pure, whatever is lovely, whatever is gracious, if there is any excellence, if there is anything worthy of praise, think about these things'), or vices (cf. e.g. Rom. 1:29ff.: 'They were filled with all manner of wickedness, evil, covetousness, malice. Full of envy, murder, strife, deceit, malignity, they are gossips, slanderers, haters of God, insolent, haughty, boastful, inventors of evil, disobedient to parents, foolish, faithless, heartless, ruthless'). Reading these codes, especially Paul's vice-lists, gives one a real flavour of the apostle's moral instruction to his converts!

A fourth category is the parenesis that arose by virtue of the need to provide encouragement to the community in particular times of distress or crisis. Whole writings, and not just individual parts, are deemed to have arisen in response to this need. We call these writings the *persecution literature*. This literature comprises our very first Gospel, the Gospel of Mark, which is deemed to have been composed either during or after the Neronian persecution of the church, or during or after the Romano–Jewish War. Another example is the First Letter of Peter, deemed to have been composed, if authentic, at the time of Emperor Nero, or, as is far more likely, either during the latter part of the reign of Domitian (90–95 CE), or during that of Trajan (98–117 CE). A third example is the Revelation of John, whose origin can be traced to the reign of Emperor Domitian (81–96 CE), but which may also incorporate visionary material emanating from the Neronian persecution. The purpose of the persecution literature was to place the earthly sufferings of the community within the total context of God's divine plan for his people.

A third internal need or activity of early Christian communities was that of discipline. There was a requirement, in other words, to produce rules for the regulation of the community. The early church needed to bring unruly members into line, to reprimand offenders against the community, to punish apostates. Again the Pauline letters offer us examples (cf. e.g. 1 Cor. 5–8 where the apostle deals with a case of incest within the Corinthian church, with lawsuits among members, with sexual matters, and with issues arising from food offered to idols), or the Gospels (cf. e.g. Mt. 16 and 18, esp. vv.15–20 where the Matthean Jesus gives instruction to the church on how to deal with offending members). As time went on, the need for more church order and organization, more fixed forms of ministry, a clearer structure, and more definite channels of authority emerged, leading to the composition of the Pastoral Epistles, for example, which are attributed to Paul but in actuality date from the late first or early second century.

If we turn now to the function of the New Testament writings vis-à-vis the world, then the first external need or activity of early Christian communities was that of *kerygma* or proclamation, missionary preaching or propaganda. The New Testament writings as a whole reflect the influence of this motivation. They were written 'out of faith, for faith'. This is especially true of the Gospels which are not objective accounts of historical facts. On the contrary, they are coloured throughout with the aim of convincing the reader of Jesus' divine person and saving work.

This is illustrated by the writer of the Fourth Gospel who is unapologetic in stating his kerygmatic purpose:

> Now Jesus did many other signs in the presence of the disciples, which are not written in this book; but these are written that you may believe that Jesus is the Christ, the Son of God, and that believing you may have life in his name (Jn 20:30–1).

Mere proclamation of one particular interpretation of Jesus' person and work often goes beyond that in the New Testament to an attack on alternative interpretations. Polemic, therefore, is another motivation for the production of the New Testament writings. The word 'polemic' comes front the Greek word *polemeo*, which means to attack or to wage war. One sees the influence of polemic, for example, in Paul's letters to the Galatians and to the Corinthians where the apostle himself attacks those who are preaching a different gospel from his own – who they are we can only guess at since history or the later church have not allowed them to speak for themselves (cf. e.g. 'But even if we, or an angel from heaven, should preach to you a gospel contrary to that which we preached to you, let him be accursed. As we have said before, so now I say again, if any one is preaching to you a gospel contrary to that which you received, let him be accursed', Gal. 1:8–9; 'For such men are false apostles, deceitful workmen, disguising themselves as apostles of Christ', 2 Cor. 11:13). The Letter of James, on the other hand, as previously noted, may represent an attack on Paul's doctrine of justification by faith or on the Paulinism which espoused it. 2 Peter and Jude, to add a further twist, are late writings which attack in turn those who criticize or pervert established Pauline teaching.

The other side of the coin from polemic is apologetic. Apologetic reflects the desire on the part of various New Testament writers or writings to defend particular versions or interpretations of the Christian faith. An *apologia* in Greek is an argument in defence or vindication of a person, cause, etc. Apologetic is to be seen, for example, in the writings of Luke–Acts. Here, we detect the desire of a predominantly Gentile–Christian church to show itself both respectable and innocuous in the eyes of the Romans. In Matthew's Gospel, by contrast, we detect the desire of a predominantly Jewish–Christian community to defend itself against its fellow Jews by affirming that it is the 'true Israel', that Jesus is the new Moses, that to its community had been given a new law. In the Johannine Epistles (1, 2 and 3 John), possibly as a result of the Gnosticizing tendency of the Fourth Gospel, we can detect the desire on the part of the later church to defend itself against Gnostics, or rather excessively Gnostic interpretations of Jesus' person and work. It was this desire, indeed, to defend itself against Gnosticism and other interpretations (branded heretical) that led more than anything else to the development of orthodoxy, a fixed canon, and the doctrine of apostolic succession. It was alternative interpretations of the tradition, especially those deemed heretical, that led to the claim of apostolic authorship for many of the New Testament writings. Heresy, therefore, was one of the major factors that led to the formation of the authoritative canon (the word means a 'rule' or 'yardstick') of twenty-seven writings now known to us as the New Testament.

We now direct our attention to the writings themselves. In what follows, I can do no more than give a general introduction, offering a classification of the writings, indicating something of their content and commenting on their dating. Specific and detailed introduction to the individual texts is something that you must follow up on your own from the many excellent and comprehensive New Testament introductions that are available.[39]

According to most New Testament commentators, the New Testament writings can be divided into three main categories. In the first place, there are the Narrative or (so-called) 'Historical' books, namely the Four Gospels (Mark, Matthew, Luke and John) and the Acts of the Apostles. In the second place, there are the Letters or 'Instruction' books. These can be further divided into four main subsections, namely the Pauline Letters, the Deutero-Pauline Literature, the Catholic Epistles and the Epistle to the Hebrews. The third category (a category of one) is the apocalyptic

Table 4 Classification of New Testament writings

Narrative or 'Historical' Books	Letters or 'Instruction' Books	Apocalyptic/Prophetic Book
The Four Gospels	**The Pauline Letters**	The Revelation of John
The Gospel according to Matthew	The Letter to the Romans	
The Gospel according to Mark	The First Letter to the Corinthians	
The Gospel according to Luke	The Second Letter to the Corinthians	
The Gospel according to John	The Letter to the Galatians	
The Acts of the Apostles	(The Letter to the Ephesians)	
	The Letter to the Philippians	
	The Letter to the Colossians	
	The First Letter to the Thessalonians	
	The Second Letter to the Thessalonians	
	The Letter of Paul to Philemon	

(Continued)

Table 4 Cont'd

Narrative or 'Historical' Books	Letters or 'Instruction' Books	Apocalyptic/Prophetic Book
	The Deutero-Pauline Literature The Letter to the Ephesians (The Letter to the Colossians) (The Second Letter to the Thessalonians) **The Pastoral Epistles** The First Letter to Timothy The Second Letter to Timothy The Letter to Titus **The Catholic Epistles** The Letter of James The Letter of Jude The First Letter of Peter The Second Letter of Peter The First Letter of John The Second Letter of John The Third Letter of John The Epistle to the Hebrews	

or prophetic book, the Revelation or Apocalypse of John. Table 4, on p. 88, makes this clearer.

The Narrative or 'Historical' Books give us accounts of how the early church viewed its past, the Gospels presenting us (as we shall see more fully in the next chapter) with edited traditions about Christianity's founder, his teaching and activity, his words and his deeds, his life and his death. The Acts of the Apostles offers, from the perspective of the sub-apostolic age, an idealized account of the origins and development of the church, from its beginnings in Jerusalem to its eventual appearance in Rome. This programme is laid out in the opening chapter when the risen Jesus addresses his disciples:

> 'But you shall receive power when the Holy Spirit has come
> upon you; and you shall be my witnesses in Jerusalem and in all
> Judea and Samaria and to the end of the earth' (Acts 1:8).

The Letters or 'Instruction' books give us a window into the church as it addresses its present concerns, the undisputed Pauline letters offering a glimpse into Christian life and witness in the communities founded by Paul in Asia Minor in the fifties; the Deutero-Pauline literature the nature of Pauline Christianity later in the century, or early in the next.

The Catholic Epistles, so-called because they are taken (a trifle erroneously) as being addressed to the church at large (rather than to specific communities as with the Pauline letters), present us with the emergent Catholicism that exerted its harmonizing influence over the final stages of New Testament Christianity, and which is characterized by a diminished eschatological concern, a corresponding salvation history perspective, an appeal to apostolic tradition and a growing institutionalism, as evinced by a preoccupation with canon, creed and clergy.

Reference was made above to the undisputed Pauline letters, as well as to the Deutero-Pauline literature. By the undisputed

Pauline letters we mean Galatians, 1 and 2 Corinthians and Romans. Most scholars would also harbour few doubts regarding authenticity with respect to 1 Thessalonians, Philippians and Philemon. 2 Thessalonians, Colossians and Ephesians, however, would be in the disputed category, with a narrow majority perhaps claiming 2 Thessalonians and Colossians as Pauline, and relegating Ephesians, together with the Pastoral Epistles (so-called because they are ostensibly written by Paul to Timothy and Titus to instruct them on their pastoral duties), to the later Deutero-Pauline literature.

The letters that make up the genuine Pauline corpus offer us a unique insight into the apostle's missionary preaching and ethical teaching. Written to communities in north or south Galatia (Derbe, Lystra, Iconium), Corinth, Philippi, Thessalonica, Colossae and Rome, they reveal Paul as a doughty champion of certain central theological tenets (the salvific nature of Christ's death and resurrection, the justification of the believer by faith, the believer's freedom over the 'principalities and powers', the law, sin and death, Christ-mysticism and the believer's incorporation into Christ, etc.) as well as a feisty defender of his own apostleship in the face of various opponents who sought to undermine his authority. The letters also provide a valuable introduction into the whole gamut of religious, moral or gender issues which plagued the early church, whether it be circumcision, meat offered to idols, factionalism, incest, sexual conduct, the role of marriage, the role of women in church, the wearing of the veil, etc.

The seven letters that make up the Catholic Epistles are the Letter of James, the Letter of Jude, the First and Second Letters of Peter, and the First, Second and Third Letters of John (the Johannine Epistles). The first four claim (falsely, as it turns out) the names of the primitive church leaders or disciples of Jesus as their authors (James and Jude, the brothers of Jesus, and the apostle Peter),[40] or, in the case of the Johannine Epistles (and the

Fourth Gospel), offer sufficient hints at a connection (with the apostle John) for later tradition to assert it with confidence.

In the case of the Epistle to the Hebrews, we have a theological treatise which, in the words of R. H. Fuller, 'is not properly speaking an "epistle" . . . is not by Paul, and . . . was not written to the "Hebrews".'[41] While it argues for the superiority of Christian institution over Jewish ones (of the new covenant, for example, over the old) or of Jesus over Moses, or over angels, or over the high priest, and while it evinces an 'interior' view of purity, and a spiritual understanding of sacrifice, the work shows, on the other hand, such a profound knowledge of, and dependence on, the Old Testament (or Hebrew Bible) that it is reasonable to assume that it was addressed to Jewish Christians who were in danger of apostasy (or merely conservatism) and were being tempted either to lapse into their original Jewish beliefs, or to remain as Christians under the umbrella of Judaism.

If the Narrative or 'Historical' books show us how the early church viewed its past, and the Letters of 'Instruction' books reveal how the church engaged with the present, the one apocalyptic or prophetic book in the New Testament, which fittingly closes the corpus, the Revelation of John, lets us see how the church envisaged its future, or rather how one persecuted, marginalized and embattled tradition within the New Testament, apocalyptic Christianity, unwilling (unlike emergent Catholicism) to compromise with the Hellenistic world, compensated for its present setbacks by conjuring up a triumphalist vision (or series of visions) of world domination. With its historical setting in a predominantly Jewish–Christian community in Asia Minor in the latter half of the first century CE, the alienated community of the Apocalypse was suffering sporadic though not necessarily systematic persecution at the hands of the Roman state and believed as a result that such persecution signalled the end of the world. The state is symbolized (conventionally) as a beast (Rev. 13:1ff.) or as a harlot (Rev. 17:1 ff.). The community itself, on the other hand, is depicted as a woman pursued by a dragon (Rev. 12:1 ff.) or as the bride of the Lamb (Rev. 19:7–8, 21:9). Behind the state's activity is that of the devil himself, symbolized by the dragon (Rev. 12:1ff.) or as a serpent (Rev. 20:21). The book was written, therefore, out of a concrete situation and for a concrete situation. It is not a prophecy of later events in world history. For the writer world history was going to end very shortly, and within his own lifetime (Rev. 1:1–3, 22:20).

Having described and categorized the New Testament writings according to the classification above, let me now make some comments on this suggested scheme. While the division of the books of the New Testament in this way is useful, other arrangements are conceivable. Since they constitute a major two-volume work, it is possible to take the Gospel of Luke and the Acts of the Apostles together as the Lukan writings. Similarly, it is possible to take the Fourth Gospel together with the three Johannine Epistles to make up the Johannine corpus of writings or the Johannine literature. The Fourth Gospel and the Johannine Epistles share a common language and style, and the latter, although they deal with the same problems as the other Catholic Epistles (the delay of the *parousia*, the question of how to be apostolic when the apostles have died, the conflict between orthodoxy and heresy, the question of how the church ought best to be governed, etc.), they all give a different answer from that given by these parallel writings. Some would also include the Revelation of John with this literature since tradition claims it to have been written by the apostle John. In my own view, however, no two writings are further apart (whether in style or in conception) than the Fourth Gospel and the Revelation of John. The latter is our best example in the New Testament of a work steeped in the ideas of apocalyptic Christianity, while the former is a supreme exemplar of a writing which has moved considerably in a Gnostic direction. While the Revelation depicts Jesus as a royal Messiah in a Jewish apocalyptic mode, the Fourth Gospel presents him quite differently as a divine Revealer with Gnostic proclivities.

One feature of the New Testament writings which is often disguised by the standard classification is the degree of inter-dependence these texts ostensibly exhibit. Matthew and Luke (and possibly John) were based on Mark, as we shall see in the next chapter. A number of the writings show the influence of Paul. The Deutero-Pauline literature was clearly based on Paul's authentic letters, and 2 Peter and Jude reflect the influence of the Pauline letters also. Luke–Acts is heir to the Pauline tradition (though Acts does not appear to have used the letters as source material).

A further feature already noted is that of pseudonymity, that is, the claim made by the writings to be written by the first disciples or those associated with them. James, 1 and 2 Peter, Jude and 1, 2 and 3 John all bear the names of apostles or relations of Jesus. Nevertheless, no New Testament writing was indisputably written by an original disciple of Jesus or by eye-witnesses of his actions or words. The majority, ironically, were written by Paul, a self-appointed apostle who had not been one of Jesus' original followers, or by writers influenced by Paul.

Let us turn now to the dating of the New Testament writings. Where the establishment of dates is concerned, the writings can be assigned to three main periods:

40–70 CE

This is the period when the early Christian movement spread into the wider Hellenistic world. The fifties, in particular, is the time when the apostle Paul was making converts and establishing communities of believers in various strategic centres in Asia Minor and Greece. This decade (50–60 CE), then, is the time-span of the undisputed Pauline Letters. Nothing in this period has come down to us, it should be noted, from the primitive church in Jerusalem or its leaders.

70–95 CE

Following on from the Fall of Jerusalem, this is a period in the church's history which is characterized by conflict, persecution, apologetic and polemic. The period is bounded by the Neronian persecution which preceded it, and the Domitianic persecution which concludes it. While continuing to expand, the church needed, nevertheless, to defend itself and its teaching in the face of considerable opposition. It needed to formulate its traditions, to promulgate them among its growing adherents, and to explain them to its emerging detractors. The writings listed below emanate from this period.

The narrative or historical writings

The Gospel according to Mark (*c.* 65–75 CE)
The Gospel according to Luke (*c.* 75–100 CE)
The Gospel according to Matthew (*c.* 75–100 CE)
The Acts of the Apostles (*c.* 80–90 CE, or perhaps later)

The persecution literature

Hebrews (*c.* 70–90 CE, or perhaps earlier)
Revelation (c. 90–95 CE)
1 Peter (*c.* 90–95, or perhaps even later in Trajan's reign 98–117 CE)

The Deutero-Pauline literature

(Colossians)
(2 Thessalonians)
Ephesians (80–95 CE, or perhaps later)

95–150 CE

With the success of the church's mission in the wider Hellenistic world comes a period of consolidation. This is the period of emergent Catholicism, a period when apologetic and polemic predominate. It is in this period that a literature dealing with church discipline, belief and conduct emerges, and the publication of an alternative more mystical, less eschatological version of the life of Jesus is seen.

The narrative or historical books

The Gospel according to John (90–110 CE)

The Deutero-Pauline literature

(Ephesians)
The Pastoral Epistles (1 and 2 Timothy, Titus) (90–120 CE)

The Catholic epistles

The Letter of James (90–140 CE)
The Letter of Jude (90–140 CE)
1 Peter (98–117 CE, or perhaps earlier, 90–95 CE)
2 Peter (125–150 CE)
1, 2 and 3 John (90–110 CE, or perhaps later)

Although these dates would command the support of most New Testament scholars, it is worth reminding ourselves of some of the differences of opinion that do prevail. Conservative scholars would regard 2 Thessalonians, Ephesians, Colossians and even the Pastorals (1 and 2 Timothy and Titus) as Pauline, while radical scholars would regard them all as Deutero-Pauline. A middle-of-the-road position, however, would probably still hold 2 Thessalonians and Colossians as the work of Paul, with Ephesians and the Pastorals by later Paulinists. Similarly, conservatives would regard Hebrews, James and Jude as early, radicals as much later.

How may we sum up this brief review of the New Testament writings? Where the church is concerned, the New Testament represents an authoritative canon against which true Christianity (and indeed all past and future developments of Christianity) is to be measured. The New Testament speaks with one voice, and that voice is the voice of the apostles bearing their witness to Jesus. One should note, however, that it was the latter half of the fourth century CE before the church finally agreed that these twenty-seven writings should constitute a definitive canon. Before this there was much controversy and dispute about what should be left in and what left out.[42]

Where the New Testament scholar is concerned, or the student of Christian origins, these writings have a different complexion. From a historical perspective, the writings may be seen as *diverse*. They reflect various traditions or viewpoints stretching over a period of one hundred years or more. They are also *incomplete*, in terms of the source material they tantalizingly allude to but which is no longer available to us. Some of Paul's letters, for example, have been lost to us (cf. e.g. 1 Cor. 5:9 where Paul refers to a previous letter he had written to the Corinthians). The primitive source of Jesus' sayings, known to us as Q, is no longer extant, and has had to be reconstructed from Matthew and Luke. Various other Gospel accounts or narratives appear to have been in existence which are similarly lost to us (cf. e.g. the sources referred to in Lk. 1: 1ff.).

Again, as we have seen, the New Testament writings, as they stand, are *not wholly representative*. There is little from original Jewish Christianity, and especially from Jesus' own immediate circle. There is nothing that can with certainty be attributed to one of his original disciples or eye-witnesses. They are also *unbalanced*. The majority of the writings are from Paul or from Paulinists, and hence are representative of Gentile Christianity, or later orthodoxy. And finally, from a historical point of view, they are *arbitrary*. A number of writings which are valuable for the reconstruction of early Christian origins, teaching and practice, and which fall within the period of the New Testament, have been left out of the canon. These include 1 Clement, the *Didache* and the Letters of Ignatius, all written at the end of the first century CE, or the beginning of the second.[43] The task of New Testament scholarship is to work with such sources and to recover, if possible, a plausible picture of Christian origins, of the historical Jesus and the early church, and it is to the tools that make such a task possible that we shall next turn.

Interpreting the Gospels: Hermeneutics

Form criticism

Thus far, we have framed this beginner's guide to the New Testament in terms of a series of ever narrowing circles. In the first chapter, we explored the world of the New Testament from the point of view of its Hellenistic and Jewish background. In the second chapter, we moved to the early church, outlining the origins and history of the first Christian communities, and examining the nature and development of belief and practice in the New Testament period. In our third chapter, we then focused on the literature produced by the early church, the New Testament writings themselves, observing how they emerged, and giving a brief introduction to them. Having presented this aerial view, I now want to dig in a particular corner of the field. In our final chapter, we shall concentrate on the three Synoptic Gospels of Matthew, Mark and Luke, but in this chapter I wish to introduce you to the tools which modern New Testament scholars employ to 'excavate' these important texts. We shall be concerned, then, with 'hermeneutics', the art (or some would even say 'science') of interpretation. The word comes from the Greek *hermeneuein* which means 'to interpret' or 'to understand', and the subject brings within its orbit all the various approaches, tools and methods which the critic brings to bear on ancient texts like the New Testament. Here, we shall only be interested in three, insofar as they relate to the Gospels, i.e. form criticism, source criticism and redaction criticism. We begin with form criticism.

In the last chapter, we saw that the majority of the New Testament writings were written after 70 CE. Prior to this, oral tradition operated in the various Christian communities. This was particularly true of the Gospels, the earliest of which was written about forty years after Jesus' death. Prior to this, various traditions about his words and deeds, his teaching and activity, his life and death circulated by word of mouth.

This fact had certain consequences. In the first place, memory played an important role in the transmission of the Jesus tradition. There is, however, a limit to what the memory can *retain*, even given the vaunted superiority of the ancient oriental mind over that of the modern age. Hence, superfluous details get forgotten as also the original order or sequence in which events happened. So, likewise, do the occasions when particular sayings or teachings were first uttered. There is a limit also to what the memory can *transmit*. What was passed on, for the most part, in the oral tradition, was no extended narrative but small, self-contained, easily memorized, separate, individual sayings or stories.

A second feature of oral tradition is the fact that it was subject to imaginative embellishment. This process can be observed at the literary level by comparing the earliest Gospel with the later ones. To enable you to do this, I have prepared another table (Table 5, overleaf) which you should consult, in conjunction with a synopsis, i.e. a work which places the text of the three Gospels in parallel columns so that they may more easily be compared and contrasted. A good example is B. H. Throckmorton's *Gospel Parallels. A Synopsis of the First Three Gospels.*[44] Let me make some comments on the examples given in this table.[45]

In the passion narratives, for example, one observes how the two nondescript mocking criminals crucified with Jesus in Mark

Table 5 Form criticism: the tendencies of the Synoptic tradition

Tendency	Example Compare (see Throckmorton, *Gospel Parallels*):
1. Imaginative embellishment	Mk 15:32 with Lk. 23:39–43 the mockers → negative/positive responses to Jesus Mk 16:1ff. with Mt. 28:1ff. and Lk. 24:1ff. one young *man* → an *earthquake/guarded tomb/ angel* → *two* men in dazzling apparel
2. Introduction of details	Mk 9:17 with Lk. 9:38 my son → my *only* son Mk 3:11 with Lk. 6:6 the withered hand → *right* hand withered Mk 14:47 with Lk. 22:50 cut off his ear → his *right* ear
3. Introduction of names	Mk 7:17 with Mt. 15:15 his disciples asked him → *Peter* said to him Mk 14:13 with Lk. 22:8 he sent two of his disciples → Jesus sent *Peter* and *John* Mk 14:47 with Jn 18:10 a *bystander* struck the high priest's *slave* → *Simon Peter. . . Malchus* Cf. also the apocryphal tradition which later supplied names for the wise men, the woman with the haemorrhage, the crucified robbers, the officer on guard at the (Matthean) tomb, etc.
4. Introduction of Opponents	Lk. 11:15 (Q) with Mk 3:22 and Mt. 12:24 crowd → scribes → Pharisees Lk. 11:16 (Q) with Mk 8:11 and Mt. 16:1 crowd → Pharisees → Pharisees and Sadducees

(Continued)

Table 5 Cont'd

Tendency	Example Compare (see Throckmorton, *Gospel Parallels*):
5. Introduction of speeches	Mk 8:32 with Mt. 16:22 began to rebuke him → began to rebuke him, saying . . . Mk 14:1 with Mt. 26:1 it was two days before → Jesus said, 'You know that after two days . . .' Mk 14:45 with Mt. 26:50 and Lk. 22:48 no reply by Jesus to Judas → 'Friend, why are you here?' → 'Judas, would you betray . . .'
6. Approximation to the Old Testament	Mk 11:2ff. with Mt. 21:2, 5–7 one colt → an *ass* and a *colt*, cf. Zech. 9:9
7. Doublets or triplets	Mk 6:34–44 with Mk 8:1–9 and Jn 6:1–14 or Mk 1:16–20 with Lk. 5:1–11 and Jn 21:1–14 same story, two/three versions Mk 11:22–23/Mt. 21:21 with Mt. 17:20 and Lk. 17:6 same saying, different forms and settings

chapter 15, verse 32 become in Luke (23:39–43) identifiable individuals representing negative and positive responses to Jesus. Likewise, in the resurrection narratives, the young man of Mark chapter 16, verse 1ff. becomes in Matthew chapter 28, verse 1ff. an angel rolling back the stone before an astonished guard who experiences an earthquake, and further, in Luke chapter 24, verse 1ff., two men in dazzling apparel.

Details absent or no longer remembered in the early tradition (represented by Mark) are supplied by the later tradition (represented by Matthew and Luke). The 'son' mentioned in the story of the deaf and dumb boy in Mark chapter 9, verse 17 becomes the father's 'only son' in Luke chapter 9, verse 38, thus lending the story more pathos. The hand of the withered man in Mark chapter 3, verse 1 is given as his 'right hand' in Luke chapter 6, verse 6, thus making the infirmity all the more serious. The chopped-off ear of the bystander in Mark chapter 14, verse 47 is his 'right ear' according to Luke chapter 22, verse 50, and the unnamed bystander himself is given the name of Malchus in the later Johannine account (Jn 18:10) with Peter himself delivering the blow.

This last feature illustrates the tendency of the later tradition to introduce proper names where the earlier one omits them. The questioning disciples of Mark chapter 7, verse 17 are replaced by Peter in Matthew's version (Mt. 15:15). The anonymous two disciples sent to arrange the upper room in Mark chapter 14, verse 13 are given as Peter and John in Luke chapter 22, verse 8. Apocryphal tradition went to even greater lengths. It supplied names for Matthew's wise men (Mt. 2:1–12), for the woman with the haemorrhage (Mk 5:25–34 par.), for the robbers crucified with Jesus and for the officer on guard at the tomb in Matthew's version of the resurrection story.

Specific categories of opponents (especially in relation to the later church) are frequently introduced where the earlier tradition had unnamed questioners. In the conflict story given in Mark chapter 3, verse 22 and par., Jesus' interlocutors are the 'crowd' in Luke's version (Lk. 11:15), which is taken to represent the earlier source, Q, the 'scribes' in Mark's version (3:22) and the 'Pharisees' in Matthew's (12:24). Likewise, Luke's 'crowd' (also Q) in chapter 11, verse 16 becomes the 'Pharisees' in Mark's version and the 'Pharisees and Sadducees' in Matthew's (16:1).

A further tendency of tradition is to introduce speeches onto the lips of the characters in stories, often by converting the indirect speech of the earlier version to direct speech. Peter is said to rebuke Jesus in Mark chapter 8, verse 32 but is given two sentences of direct speech when Matthew takes over his source ('And Peter began to rebuke him saying, "God forbid, Lord! This shall never happen to you"', 16:22). Mark's statement that 'it was now two days before the Passover and the feast of Unleavened Bread' is rendered as direct speech on the lips of Jesus in Matthew chapter 26, verse 1 ('Jesus said, "You know that after two days the Passover is coming . . ." '). Unable to resist the dramatic impact of Judas's betrayal of Jesus with a kiss in the garden of Gethsemane, both Matthew and Luke issue Jesus with two separate but equally suitable rejoinders, 'Friend, why are you here?' (Mt. 26:50) and 'Judas, would you betray the Son of Man with a kiss?' (Lk. 22:48).

Where suggestive parallels occurred in the Old Testament (or Hebrew Bible), the later tradition was not averse to conforming its Jesus tradition even more exactly to the sacred text, or using that text to furnish other details. Mark, for example, has Jesus enter Jerusalem on an ass, but Matthew, writing with Zechariah chapter 9, verse 9 in mind ('Lo, your king comes to you; triumphant and victorious is he, humble and riding on an ass, on a colt the foal of an ass') has him enter on an ass *and* a colt, in a manoeuvre that one critic has likened to a circus act!

One further feature of the oral transmission of tradition is the tendency for more than one version of a saying or story to develop, or in other words, the emergence of what critics call 'doublets', or even 'triplets'. Mark offers his readers what appear to be two versions of the same story, the feeding of the multitude (6:34–44 and 8:1–9), and John offers us another (Jn 6:1–14). The story of the call of the disciples in Mark chapter 1, verses 16–20, with its climactic words 'I shall make you fishers of men', is found again in an embellished form (as a miracle story) in Luke chapter 5, verses 1–11, and yet again, in a different (post-resurrection) context, in John chapter 21, verses 1–14. The mountain-moving saying of Mark chapter 11, verses 22–23 is also found in different forms and settings in Matthew chapter 21, verse 21; chapter 17, verse 20 and Luke chapter 17, verse 6.

Having observed some of the ways that the sayings and stories of Jesus were embellished as they were passed on, let us now consider the function which these oral traditions of his words and deeds played in the communities which transmitted them. We have seen that memory played a role in the transmission of the core tradition, but that imaginative embellishment was likewise exercised upon it. It is worth emphasizing, however, that the memory exercised by the early church on its tradition was not arbitrary but selective. Each saying or story was remembered and transmitted if it served the needs or purposes of a particular Christian community – if it had a *function*, in other words. The needs or activities of early Christian communities were described in our last chapter, and you may wish to recall these: worship (liturgy), parenesis, *didache*, catechesis, discipline, *kerygma*, polemic, apologetic.

Each saying or story was remembered and transmitted if it shed light on the church's worship – that is, if it had a *liturgical* function. It was remembered and transmitted if it edified, exhorted, encouraged believers – that is, if it had a *parenetical* function. It was remembered and transmitted if it was useful in the teaching of church members – that is, if it had a *didactic* function. It was remembered and transmitted if it was useful for the instruction of catechumens – that is, if it had a *catechetical* function. It was remembered and transmitted if it served the needs of church order and organization – that is, if it had a *disciplinary* function. Each saying or story was remembered and transmitted if it was useful for missionary preaching or sermon illustration – that is, if it had a *kerygmatic* function. It was remembered and transmitted if it supplied ammunition against the community's opponents or helped defend a particular interpretation of Jesus' life or death – that is, if it had a *polemical* or *apologetic* function.

By virtue of the fact that each story or saying performed, then, a certain *function* within the *life-situation* or *setting* of the early church – even though it may have had its origin in the ministry of Jesus – it came to be shaped, moulded, or influenced by the purpose it served. The individual units of tradition adopted a form appropriate to their function. If they were used for worship, they adopted a liturgical form in the oral tradition. If they were used for teaching, they took a shape best suited for that purpose. If they were used in preaching, they were honed down or adapted for effective sermon illustration. Here, the setting was less important than the teaching (or punchline) enshrined in the unit. If they were used in making Gentile converts, then, conversely, they tended to emphasize the details which vaunted Jesus' superiority as a miracle-worker over other Hellenistic wonder-workers, heroes or gods.

As a result, the individual units within the Gospel tradition are to be found in a variety of specific and identifiable 'forms'. In some cases you find a unit with a brief and variable narrative setting which enshrines an important saying (critics call this an apophthegm, a paradigm or a pronouncement story). You also find proverbs, aphorisms, parables, miracle stories, legends, etc.

These forms adopted by the pre-Gospel or pre-Synoptic tradition, and incorporated into the Gospels, are not unique. The material has certain standard or conventional features which can be recognized also in Jewish, Hellenistic and other folk traditions. Sometimes they are even borrowed and transferred to Jesus from other traditions (e.g. the wine miracle at Cana from the Dionysiac miracle tradition).

There is yet one further consequence of the 'functional' nature of oral tradition. By constant use and repetition in their particular setting, and in response to their particular function, the individual units of oral tradition became rounded off and polished. Superfluous historical or eye-witness details not serving any particular purpose were forgotten. Awkward corners or edges were knocked off. They became vivid, concise, streamlined for the purpose they served. The stories or sayings about Jesus 'pursued their way', as one critic, the late W. D. Davies, has observed, like 'pebbles in a stream'.[46] Another image suggested for them is 'pearls' or 'beads', each valuable in its own way. It was these 'pearls' or beads' (which form critics call 'pericopae') that the evangelists collected and supplied with a string. And it is the combination of these beads or pearls and the string, or the isolated units of tradition (pericopae) together with their editorial framework which, with some modifications, make up the structure of our Gospels.

This recognition of the nature of the Gospels and of the character of the oral tradition prior to their compilation came as a result of the work of the form critics. The study of folk tradition or of secular folklore had gone on since the nineteenth century and had been first applied in other fields outside the Bible. It was then applied to the Old Testament (or Hebrew Bible) by H. Gunkel. Form criticism of the New Testament is associated with the names of three German scholars, K. L. Schmidt, M. Dibelius, R. Bultmann and one British scholar, V. Taylor.

K. L. Schmidt was the first to recognize the 'pearls/string' pattern in Mark's Gospel, or 'unit structure'. He published his findings in 1919 in a book called *Der Rahmen der Geschichte Jesu* ('The Framework of the history of Jesus').[47] Schmidt claimed that the Gospel consisted of a whole series of separate units (pericopae) which were linked by a loose, wholly artificial, geographical and chronological framework. The only exception was the passion narrative. The 'pearls', he asserted, moreover, could be separated from the string.

Dibelius' book, *Die Formgeschichte des Evangeliums* (translated into English, and published in 1934 as *From Tradition to Gospel*), also appeared in 1919. Dibelius isolated and classified the main units or 'pearls': paradigm ('a short illustrative notice or story of an event, not more descriptive than is necessary to make the point for the sake of which it is introduced'), parenesis (material that is hortatory or exhortative in nature), *Novelle* (his word for the miracle story), legend ('a narrative about some sainted person') and myth ('a story which deals with a *particular* relation and action of a god'). The main influence in the oral period producing the distinctive 'forms' of the traditional material was, he claimed, the preaching activity of the church ('In the beginning was the sermon'). The material had taken the form it had because of its function in preaching. Preaching was its life-setting or creative milieu, its *sitz im leben*.

Bultmann published his *Die Geschichte der synoptischen Tradition* (translated into English, and published in 1963 as *The History of the Synoptic Tradition*) in 1921. He offered a more elaborate, and more enduring, classification of the separate units of tradition (pericopae). He suggested a wider number and a greater variety of *sitz im leben*. He claimed, moreover, that much of the traditional material had been created, rather than merely transmitted, by the early church to serve its needs. Taylor, the author of *The Formation of the Gospel Tradition* (1933), was less sceptical than Bultmann, on the other hand, about the possibility of Gospel traditions going back to Jesus himself.

But how do we determine what might go back to Jesus himself? Form-critical method posits three main steps or operations. Starting from the texts as they are before us (rather than from assumptions, however plausible, about what must have happened in Jesus' lifetime), it works its way back analytically. The first step is to recover the traditional units from the editorial work of the evangelists and to classify these according to their form. The second step is to determine the particular function this material may have had in the early church. In what context was it transmitted? What interest or concern of the early church is likely to have led to its creation or preservation? The third step is to assess the historical value of the material, i.e. its value in throwing light on Jesus' life. If created by the church, it still has historical value in that it would then throw light on the Christian community. If the work of the later evangelists, it too would have historical value except that this time it would throw light on the concerns of the writers. From a knowledge of the way that the folk tradition transmits oral material, and from a knowledge of the theological and other concerns of the later church, form critics set out to determine the extent of development that a particular unit of tradition has undergone. In their searches for the historical Jesus, form critics seek to peel away, therefore, the embellishments or accretions of later tradition. They attempt to remove, one might say, the outer husk of the tradition, to get at the historical 'nut' within. Unkind critics, of course, have offered the 'onion' as a better analogy than the 'nut'. You peel and peel but find yourself with nothing left (but tears)!

Such total scepticism is unjustified. The methods applied by New Testament scholars in their quest for the historical Jesus are not wholly arbitrary or subjective. Certain criteria have been established to enable us to determine what has a high probability of coming from the primary level of the tradition (i.e. Jesus' lifetime), and what has a low probability and is likely to be later accretion. Four criteria of authenticity (in respect of Jesus' sayings in particular) can be mentioned:

The first criterion is the criterion of dissimilarity or distinctiveness. Something attributed to Jesus is more likely to be authentic (or 'dominical' in the language of the classic form critics) if it stands out, opposes, shows its distinctiveness, first, over against what we know of contemporary Judaism – Jesus wasn't crucified or didn't incur Jewish antipathy merely for repeating the truisms of Jewish folklore or wisdom – and second, over against what we know of later Christianity – if it reflects what we can determine, on other grounds, is the product of later developments in Christian belief and practice, then we are entitled to be suspicious that it has been falsely attributed to him. On these grounds, the harsh saying 'Let the dead bury their dead' (Mt. 8:21–22) is likely to be authentic, since it is unparalleled in ancient tradition, and goes against both Jewish, Hellenistic and Christian norms of behaviour. Likewise, the datum that Jesus was not an ascetic, and did not fast (Mk 2:19) is likely to be authentic, since the later church adopted fasting from Judaism.

Jesus' eschatological sayings (i.e. those predicting the new age) stand a strong chance of being authentic since the early church would hardly have invented them given that the kingdom of God, and especially the *parousia*, did not occur in their lifetime.

A second criterion is that of multiple attestation or the cross-section method. If a saying or story appears in two or more sources which are independent of one another (e.g. Mark and Q), then we are entitled to conclude that that saying or story is earlier than the sources in which it occurs.

A third criterion is the criterion of authentic context, or what other critics have described as the linguistic or environmental criterion. If a saying or story fits easily into the context of Jesus' own life, if it exhibits Aramaic traits (i.e. of language, or of poetic form – or even if it can be easily translated back into Aramaic), or a knowledge of Palestinian conditions is reflected in it, it is more likely to be early than late. Jesus' address to God in Mark chapter 14, verse 36 ('*Abba*, Father') or his *Amen* sayings (i.e. those introduced by the formula 'Truly, I say to you', e.g. Mk 9:1 or 11:23 and par.) have been counted as examples.

A final criterion is the criterion of consistency (C. E. Carlston) or coherence. Other traditions in the Gospels are more likely to be authentic than not, if they are consistent with the central message of Jesus, namely, the assured minimum of genuine material as determined by the application of the above criteria.

The form-critical method, then, involves the classification of the forms, the establishment of their *sitz im leben*, and the assessment of their historical value. What are the main forms of the Synoptic tradition? What are the *sitze im leben* suggested for them? I will briefly summarize these, but fuller details are to be found in the accompanying tables (Tables 6 and 7 pp. 111–118) along with examples. These you should go over carefully, preferably with a synopsis. The classification for the most part follows that of Bultmann.[48] Bultmann divided the Synoptic tradition into two main groupings, the Sayings tradition and the Narrative tradition.

Table 6 The forms of the Synoptic tradition (sayings)

Name/Term	Definition	Formal Characteristics	Examples	Sitz im leben	Historical Assessment
1. apophthegms = paradigms = pronouncement stories	sayings with a brief narrative setting	narrative setting vague and imprecise; framework provides only the situation in which saying was spoken and its occasion; few additional details; interest focuses on saying as 'punchline' at the end; occasion may be the question of a disciple or opponent which the saying answers	Mk 2:16–17, 2:18–19, 2:23–28, 10:13–15, 11:27–33, Lk. 17:20–1	preaching (Dibelius); preaching, apologetic and polemic (Bultmann)	disputed; framework for saying sometimes constructed by church/evangelist; those with characteristically Jewish question-counter-question format probably formulated in a Jewish environment (Bultmann); Hellenistic apophthegms tend to have introductory formula 'when he was asked by', 'once when he observed how'; cf. e.g. Lk. 17:20–21
2. wisdom sayings	proverbs or aphorisms embodying conventional wisdom	short, pithy, epigrammatic; in the form of general principles, exhortations or questions	Mk 9:40, 49, 10:9, 31, Mt. 6:27, 34b, 12:34b, 22:14, 24:28, Lk. 4:23, 5:39, 6:31	parenesis	majority of wisdom sayings have a parallel in Jewish and oriental literature generally; cf. e.g. Lk. 14:7–11 with Prov. 25:6–7; strong possibility that many have been borrowed, therefore, from the treasure of Jewish proverbial lore (Bultmann)

(Continued)

Table 6 Cont'd

Name/Term	Definition	Formal Characteristics	Examples	Sitz im leben	Historical Assessment
3. prophetic/ apocalyptic sayings	predictions; warnings of impending crisis; summonses to repentance; admonitions; promises of future reward	'distinguished by their brevity and vigour' (Bultmann); blessing/ woe formula employed; antithetical structure common	Mk 9:1, 10:29–30, 13:5–27; Mt. 23; Lk. 6:20–26 = Mt. 5:3–12; Lk. 10:23–24 = Mt. 13:16–17; Lk. 14:15	preaching, parenesis, polemic	strong possibility that many may go back to Jesus, though some would appear to be community formations or *Gemeindebildungen*; cf. e.g. Rev. 1:17–18, 3:20, 16:15 (derived from Christian prophets?)
4. legal sayings/ community rules	sayings expressing Jesus' attitude to the Law/ sayings setting forth the regulations of the community	conditional clause (when/if…) followed by an imperative/ assertion or 'whoever …' formula common; antithetical structure also common	Mk 2:27, 7:15, 10:11–12, 11:25= Mt. 6:14–15; Mt. 5:21–22, 27–28, 33–37, 6:2–4, 16–18; Mk 10:42–5; Mt. 16:18–19, 18:15–22, 23:8–10	apologetic, polemic, parenesis, esp. discipline	disputed; legal sayings which have a parallel in the preaching of the OT prophets against external piety may well go back to Jesus; community rules almost certainly originated in the early church (Bultmann)

(Continued)

Table 6 Cont'd

Name/Term	Definition	Formal Characteristics	Examples	Sitz im leben	Historical Assessment
5. Christological sayings	sayings reflecting an understanding of Jesus' person and work	'I-sayings' in which Jesus speaks about the purpose of his coming, his relationship with God, his passion and resurrection	Mk 2:17b, 10:45b; Mt. 10:34–36 = Lk. 12:51– 53; Mt. 11:25–27 = Lk. 10:21–22; Mt. 18:20; cf. esp. 'Son of Man' sayings, e.g. Mk 2:10, 28; Mt. 8:20; Lk. 19:10; passion predictions Mk 8:31,9:31; 10:33–34; 'I am' sayings of John's Gospel, e.g. Jn 6:35, 8:12,11:25, etc.	various	by virtue of their reflective and retrospective point of view, there is a high probability that most of these are church formulations; they express the Christology of the believing Christian community, particularly that of the Hellenistic churches (Bultmann)

(Continued)

Table 6 Cont'd

Name/Term	Definition	Formal Characteristics	Examples	Sitz im leben	Historical Assessment
6. parables	sayings or stories from everyday life and nature upon which the hearer is usually invited to make a judgement and then apply that judgement to him or herself	as originally conceived, intended to convey one main point, or intended to make one point or truth clear (Jülicher); colourful details from everyday life serve merely to further this aim (like feathers on an arrow)	Mk 4; Mt. 13; Lk. 15–16	preaching, parenesis, esp. teaching and catechesis, apologetic, polemic	high probability that most go back to Jesus in some form; abundant signs of allegorization, however, indicate much overlay from later tradition; cf. e.g. Mk 12:1–12; application is usually secondary; cf. e.g. Mk 4:10–20; Mt. 22:11–14; Lk. 18:6–8

Table 7 The forms of the Synoptic tradition (narrative)

Name/Term	Definition	Formal Characteristics	Examples	Sitz im leben	Historical Assessment
1. miracle stories/tales *Wundergeschichten* (Bultmann)/ *Novellen* (Dibelius)	stories in which the main point of interest is the display of miraculous power; basic types: nature miracles, healing miracles, exorcisms, raisings from the dead	(a) details important (contrast apophthegms); exhibit 'pleasure in the narrative itself' (Dibelius) (b) basic three-fold structure: 1) the condition of the patient recounted; 2) the healing narrated; 3) the cure described (c) common motifs/emphases (under each section): 1) gravity, duration of illness emphasized; futility of past efforts to cure; miracle-worker received with scorn, etc.; 2) magical manipulations of miracle-worker described; use of touch, spittle, etc.; uttering of magical formula, usually in foreign language; absence of witnesses at time of healing itself, etc.; 2) the healing/exorcism visibly demonstrated by some action on part of patient (taking up bed, walking, etc.), the demon (entry into another subject/object – statue, herd of pigs, etc.) or otherwise; astonished reaction of crowd (the 'amazement' motif)	Mk 1.29–31, 4.37–41, 5.1–43, 6.45–52, 7.31–37, 8.1–9, 8.22–26, 9.14–27	apologetic, polemic	of doubtful historicity; show features common to other Jewish and particularly Hellenistic miracle stories (where miracle-worker is shown to be an epiphany or manifestation of God); most originated, according to Bultmann, in a Hellenistic milieu, and were designed to prove Jesus' superiority over rival miracle-workers, divine-men and gods.

(Continued)

Table 7 Cont'd

Name/Term	Definition	Formal Characteristics	Examples	Sitz im leben	Historical Assessment
2. legends	lit. 'that which ought to be read' (Latin *legere* = to read); technically, a story connected with the life/death of a holy man, saint or martyr and designed to be read (in mediaeval times) on the day on which he was commemorated; term applied by Dibelius to certain stories in the Gospels	none to speak of (many dispute this category, therefore); character better defined by purpose/function (stories often designed to elevate virtues/deplore vices of significant characters in the tradition as positive/negative examples to believers) or by content (display common folklore conventions, e.g. portents/miracles surround birth/life/death; precocity in youth; gifts of clairvoyance/omniscience, oratory, miracle-working predicated, etc.)	Mk 11:1–11 and par.; 14:12–16 and par.; Lk. 2:41–49; Mt. 14:28–33; Acts 1:15–20/ Mt. 27:3–10	preaching, worship, parenesis	difficult to evaluate since form little guide; tradition criticism (rather than form criticism) a better tool

Table 7 Cont'd

Name/Term	Definition	Formal Characteristics	Examples	Sitz im leben	Historical Assessment
3. myths	narratives where 'the supernatural is seen breaking in upon the human scene' (Travis)	none to speak of (hence many also dispute this category); character better defined by content (common motifs: cosmic language, reference to angels, demons, and other supernatural beings, esp. Satan; split heavens; supernatural voices; characters able to levitate or be metamorphosed, etc.	Mk 1:9–11 and par.; 1:12–13 and par.; 9:2–8 and par.	worship?	difficult to evaluate since form of itself again little guide to historicity; relation to myth/history a wider issue than form criticism can answer
4. passion narrative	the narrative account of Jesus' suffering and death	acknowledged by earlier form critics as the only type of narrative material issuing from the oral period to have existed in a longer, more continuous narrative form	Mk 14:32–15:47 and par.	worship, preaching, apologetic	more recent studies indicate passion narrative itself is composite, i.e. it comprises separate pericopae or clusters of pericopae brought together more so by the evangelists than by the tradition before them;

(Continued)

Table 7 Cont'd

Name/Term	Definition	Formal Characteristics	Examples	Sitz im leben	Historical Assessment
			longer versions said to include the institution of the Lord's Supper (Mk 14:1ff. and par.) or even the whole of Jesus' final visit to Jerusalem (Mk 11:1ff. and par.)		passion narrative not an historical transcript but also kerygmatic; several motivations colour the presentation, namely the desire to show that Jesus died as Messiah, that his death was a vicarious atonement for sin, that his passion and death were the fulfilment of OT prophecies (Fuller)

The main forms of the Sayings tradition are apophthegms, wisdom sayings, prophetic or apocalyptic sayings, legal sayings and community rules, Christological sayings and parables. The main forms of the Narrative tradition are miracle stories, legends, myths, the passion narrative. Bultmann groups categories two and three of the Narrative tradition (Dibelius' categories), that is, legends and myths, under the heading 'historical stories and legends'.

The first and most prominent of the forms in the Sayings tradition is what Bultmann calls the apophthegm, Dibelius the paradigm and Taylor the pronouncement story. These terms describe a saying with a brief narrative setting. Their creative milieu or *sitz im leben*, according to Dibelius, was preaching, to which Bultmann added apologetic and polemic. While the embedded saying was probably authentic, the framework (which frequently varies in the triple tradition) was more often than not secondary.

The following are three examples. In the first, you should note the vagueness of the narrative framework (we are not told, for example, who 'they' were) and the kingdom of God saying which acts as the punchline to the unit. In the second and (closely related) third, you should observe again the brief narrative setting, the question–counter-question format (typical of Jewish apophthegms) and the sayings forming the climax of each unit.

And they were bringing children to him, that he might touch them; and the disciples rebuked them. But when Jesus saw it he was indignant, and said to them, 'Let the children come to me, do not hinder them; for to such belongs the kingdom of God' (Mk 10:13–15).

And the scribes of the Pharisees, when they saw that he was eating with sinners and tax collectors, said to his disciples, 'Why does he eat with tax collectors and sinners?' And when Jesus heard it, he said to them, 'Those who are well have no need of a physician, but those who are sick' . . . Now John's disciples and the Pharisees were fasting; and people came and said to him, 'Why do John's disciples and the disciples of the Pharisees fast, but your disciples do not fast?' And Jesus said to them, 'Can the wedding guests fast while the bridegroom is with them?' (Mk 2:16–17; 18–19).

A second form is the wisdom (or gnomic) saying. These sayings are proverbs or aphorisms embodying conventional wisdom. They are frequently brief, pithy or epigrammatic, as the examples which follow show. Used to instruct or exhort, their *sitz im leben* was parenesis. Since they are almost all paralleled in Jewish wisdom literature, none of them requires to be seen as unique to Jesus, according to Bultmann, and hence distinctive of him, although this judgement is being revised today. A number of the wisdom sayings were probably borrowed, he claimed, by the church from the treasure of Jewish proverbial lore.

Let the day's own trouble be sufficient for the day (Mt. 6:34b).
For out of the abundance of the heart the mouth speaks (Mt. 12:34b).
And as you wish that men would do to you, do so to them (Lk. 6:31).

A third category of Jesus' reported sayings are the prophetic or apocalyptic sayings. These include predictions, warnings of impending crisis, summonses to repentance, admonitions, promises of future reward. They are frequently couched in the future tense, often exhibit an antithetical structure (that is, two parallel statements, the second of which offers a contrast) and may involve a blessing or woe formula. Preaching, polemic and apologetic are their suggested *sitz im leben*. Many probably go back to Jesus himself, although some may be the product of Christian prophets. The following passage offers an example. Note the rhythm of the sayings and the series of contrasts (blessed are you . . . woe to you; hunger . . . satisfied . . . weep . . . laugh, etc.):

Blessed are you poor, for yours is the kingdom of God.

Blessed are you that hunger now, for you shall be satisfied.

Blessed are you that weep now, for you shall laugh . . .

But woe to you that are rich, for you have received your consolation.

Woe to you that are full now, for you shall hunger.

Woe to you that laugh now, for you shall mourn and weep (Lk. 6:20–6).

The next category are the legal sayings and the community rules. The former are sayings purporting to express Jesus' attitude to the Jewish law (hand-washing before meals, sabbath observance, the food laws, almsgiving, prayer, fasting, divorce, etc.). The latter are sayings which set forth regulations for the community. The legal sayings which exhibit a strong prophetic stamp may go back to Jesus, but the community rules are almost certainly *community formations* or, what Bultmann termed *Gemeindebildungen*. The following are examples. Note again the rhythm of the sayings, and their antithetical structure, and in the case of the third, a community rule, the obviously anachronistic use of the word 'church' on Jesus' lips.

The sabbath was made for man, not man for the sabbath (Mk 2:27).

You have heard that it was said to the men of old, 'You shall not kill; and whoever kills shall be liable to judgement.' But I say to you that every one who is angry with his brother shall be liable to judgement; whoever insults his brother shall be liable to the council, and whoever says, 'You fool!' shall be liable to the hell of fire (Mt. 5:21–22).

If your brother sins against you, go and tell him his fault, between you and him alone. If he listens to you, you have gained your brother. But if he does not listen, take one or two others along with you, that every word may be confirmed by the evidence of two or three witnesses. If he refuses to listen to them, tell it to the church; and if he refuses to listen even to the church, let him be to you as a Gentile and a tax collector (Mt. 18:15–20).

A further class of sayings are the Christological sayings. As their name implies, these are sayings which reflect an understanding or interpretation of Jesus' person and mission. They are frequently in the 'I' form, and make statements about the purpose of Jesus' coming, his relationship with God, or his future death or resurrection. These sayings exhibit a reflective or retrospective point of view. They are relatively infrequent in the Synoptic Gospels, but as the tradition advances they become more explicit and more numerous, as the developing Christology and soteriology of the believing Christian community is placed progressively on Jesus' lips. The supreme example of these is to be found in the famous 'I am' sayings of the Fourth Gospel. Examples include:

I came not to call the righteous, but sinners (Mk 2:17b).

The Son of Man came not to be served, but to serve, and to give his life as a ransom for many (Mk 10:45b).

The Son of Man will be delivered to the chief priests and the scribes, and they will condemn him to death, and deliver him to the Gentiles; and they will mock him, and spit upon him, and scourge him, and kill him; and after three days he will rise (Mk 10:33–34).

I am the bread of life (Jn 6:35)
I am the light of the world (Jn 8:12)
I am the good shepherd (Jn 10:11)
I am the resurrection and the life (Jn 11:25)
I am the way, and the truth, and the life (Jn 14:6).

One final, easily recognized and extremely significant element of the Sayings tradition is the parables that are attributed to Jesus.

Parables are stories from everyday life with one main point of comparison upon which hearers are invited to make a judgement and then apply that judgement to themselves. In this respect, they are different from allegories, which are more elaborate stories, whose numerous details have a veiled meaning, and which are often artificial as a result. Parables come in three main forms, the parabolic saying, the similitude and the narrative parable. An example of each of these is given below. Note the single image which characterizes the first, the comparison formula, the extended image and the series of verbs in the present tense that characterizes the second, and the full story told in the past tense that characterizes the third. Most of the parables are probably dominical in some form but few have not suffered subsequent allegorization in the course of their transmission, and, since their original point was often lost by the time they came to be written down, the applications frequently attached to them (e.g. Mk 4:10–20; Mt. 22:11–13; Lk. 18:6–8) are generally regarded as secondary.

Is a lamp brought in to be put under a bushel, or under a bed, and not on a stand? (Mk 4:21).

And he said, 'The kingdom of God is as if a man should scatter seed upon the ground, and should sleep and rise night and day, and the seed should sprout and grow, he knows not how. The earth produces of itself, first the blade, then the ear, then the full grain in the ear. But when the grain is ripe, at once he puts in the sickle, because the harvest has come' (Mk 4:26–29).

Listen! A sower went out to sow. And as he sowed, some seed fell along the path, and the birds came and devoured it. Other seed fell on rocky ground, where it had not much soil, and immediately it sprang up, since it had no depth of soil; and when the sun rose it was scorched, and since it had no root it withered away. Other seed fell among thorns and the thorns grew up and choked it and it yielded no grain, and other seeds fell into good soil and brought forth grain, growing up and increasing and yielding thirtyfold and sixtyfold and a hundred-fold (Mk 4:3–8).

According to classical form criticism, the forms of the Narrative tradition comprise miracle stories, legends, myths (or historical stories and legends, Bultmann), and the passion narrative. Miracle stories are tales (exorcisms, healings, nature miracles, raisings from the dead) in which the main point of interest lies in the miraculous display of power. Here, the details are important, in contrast to the apophthegm (or paradigm/pronouncement story) whose brevity of narrative description was noted above. Miracle stories, such as the example given below, normally possess a three-fold structure in which a) the condition of the patient is recounted; b) the healing is narrated and c) the cure is described. Common motifs or descriptive conventions which elaborate this structure, include the gravity or duration of the illness, the futility of past efforts to effect a cure, the scorn directed at the miracle-worker on his appearance, the magical manipulations employed (the use of touch, spittle, the uttering of a magic formula, etc.), the absence of witnesses at the specific time of healing, the visible proof that the cure has taken place, the astonished reaction of the crowd and so on. Evincing features common to Jewish and especially Hellenistic miracle stories, Bultmann claimed that the miracle stories attributed to Jesus in the Gospel tradition were of doubtful historicity. Originating in a mostly Hellenistic milieu, and designed to prove Jesus' superiority over rival miracle-workers, divine men and gods, they were apologetic and polemical in function. This view, too, is being revised, recent Historical Jesus studies serving to confirm the view that Jesus' reputation may originally have been founded on the fact that he was a powerful healer and exorcist, however much the miracle tradition associated with him was the product of 'creative storytelling' or embellishment.

> Now Simon's mother-in-law lay sick with a fever, and immediately they told him of her. And he came and took her by the hand and lifted her up, and the fever left her; and she served them (Mk 1:30–31).

Legends are technically stories connected with a saint, holy man or martyr which are designed to be read (Latin: *legere/legenda*) on the day on which he (or she) was commemorated. The term was applied by Dibelius to certain stories in the Gospels (e.g. Mk 11:1–11 par., 14:12–16; Lk. 2:41–49; Mt. 14:28–33; Acts 1:15–20 = Mt. 27:3–8). Legends lack the more formal structure of miracle stories (and hence some dispute that they can be considered a 'form' as such) but, like miracle stories they demonstrate certain recurrent motifs or conventions; for example, the portents or miracles surrounding the birth, life or death of the hero or villain, the hero's precocity when young, the gifts of clairvoyance, omniscience, oratory, miracle-working, etc. predicated of him and so on.

The character of legends is defined by either their *content* (common folklore conventions) or their *function*. They were clearly designed to edify believers by holding up certain virtues for them to emulate, or certain vices for them to avoid or deplore. Legends are difficult to evaluate on purely form-critical grounds, therefore, and a number of scholars believe that tradition criticism (that branch of historical criticism which makes a critical examination of the development of traditions) is a better tool with which to analyse them. Two Gospel legends are given below, each demonstrating the opposing poles of virtue and vice:

> Now his parents went to Jerusalem every year at the feast of the Passover. And when he was twelve years old, they went up according to custom; and when the feast was ended, as they were returning, the boy Jesus stayed behind in Jerusalem. His parents did not know it, but supposing him to be in the company they went a day's journey, and they sought him among their kinsfolk and acquaintances; and when they did not find

him, they returned to Jerusalem seeking him. After three days they found him in the temple sitting among the teachers, listening to them and asking them questions; and all who heard him were amazed at his understanding and his answers. And when they saw him they were astonished; and his mother said to him, 'Son, why have you treated us so? Behold, your father and I have been looking for you anxiously.' And he said to them, 'How is it that you sought me? Did you not know that I must be in my Father's house?' (Lk. 2:41–49)

When Judas, his betrayer, saw that he was condemned, he repented and brought back the thirty pieces of silver to the chief priests and the elders, saying, 'I have sinned in betraying innocent blood.' They said, 'What is that to us? See to it yourself.' And throwing down the pieces of silver in the temple, he departed; and he went and hanged himself. But the chief priests, taking the pieces of silver, said, 'It is not lawful to put them into the treasury, since they are blood money.' So they took counsel, and bought with them the potter's field, to bury strangers in. Therefore that field has been called the Field of Blood to this day (Mt. 27:3–8; cf. Acts 1:15–20).

Another problematic form, identified by Dibelius but avoided by other form critics, is myth, a narrative 'in which the supernatural is seen breaking in upon human scene'.[49] Dibelius cited only three narratives which conformed to this category (Mk 1:9–11 par.; Mt. 4:1–11 par.; Mk 9:2–8 par.). Again, 'myths' are difficult to approach from a purely form critical point of view since their formal characteristics are difficult to determine, and any analysis of them involves a judgement on the ancient 'world-view'. In the example below, you should note the cosmic language, the reference to the split heavens, the Spirit descending like a dove, the supernatural voice from heaven, the confrontation of Jesus with Satan in the wilderness, the presence of angels, etc.

In those days Jesus came from Nazareth of Galilee and was baptized by John in the Jordan. And when he came up out of the water, immediately he saw the heavens opened and the Spirit descending upon him like a dove; and a voice came from heaven, 'Thou art my beloved Son; with thee I am well pleased.'

The Spirit immediately drove him out into the wilderness. And he was in the wilderness forty days, tempted by Satan; and he was with the wild beasts; and the angels ministered to him (Mk 1:9–11, 12–13).

The so-called 'passion narrative' is the name given to the narrative of Jesus' arrest, trial, crucifixion and death (Mk 14:32–15:47 and par.), or to the longer version which includes the last supper (14:1ff. and par.) of even Jesus' final visit to Jerusalem (Mk 11:1ff. and par.) This is the only type of narrative material which was acknowledged by the earlier form critics to have existed in the oral period in a longer, more continuous form. Recent studies indicate, however, that this may not be the case and that the passion narrative, as with other sections of the Gospel of Mark, is composite, that is, it was compiled by the evangelist out of separate traditions (e.g. the betrayal by Judas, the anointing of Jesus, the institution of the eucharist, etc.). The narrative itself is not a historical transcript, but shows abundant signs, as R. H. Fuller has pointed out, of also being *kerygmatic*. The text reveals to its readers an obvious desire to show that Jesus died as the Messiah, that his death was salvific (cf. Mk 14:24), and that the events surrounding his death fulfilled Old Testament prophecies (cf. e.g. Mk 14:18 and Ps. 41:9; Mk 14:27 and Zech. 13:7 and the numerous parallels between the account of the crucifixion itself and Ps. 22).

Form criticism has been a useful tool for the historian, and has been applied to the other writings of the New Testament. Where the Pauline Letters and Deutero-Pauline literature are concerned, it has identified and highlighted the use of such forms as doxologies (e.g. Rom. 11:36, 16:25–27), benedictions (e.g. 2 Cor. 13:14), creeds and confessions (e.g. 1 Cor. 12:3; 1 Tim. 3:16), hymns (e.g. Phil. 2:6–11; Col. 1:15–20), virtue-lists (e.g. Phil. 4.8; Gal. 5:22–23), vice-lists (e.g. Rom. 1:29–31; Gal. 5:19–21) and household codes (e.g. Col. 3:18–4:1; Eph. 5:22–6:9). Similar forms have been detected in the Catholic Epistles (see e.g. the household code in 1 Pet. 2:18–3:7, the doxology in 2 Pet. 3:18b or the confession of 1 Jn 4:2–3). In the Revelation of John, too, one can find such forms, many of them with a distinctive apocalyptic flavour (cf. e.g. the benediction of 1:4, the letters of 2:1–3:22, the doxologies of 4:8 or 4:11, the hymns of 11:17–18 or 15:3–4).

Although form criticism has contributed much in particular to our understanding of the tradition behind the Gospels, and to our knowledge of the interests and concerns of the communities which produced them, the reception of the discipline among English-speaking scholarship on the whole has been to some extent unsympathetic, largely on account of the scepticism of its results vis-à-vis the tracing back of historical data to Jesus' lifetime.[50]

Conservative critics have queried whether a span of forty years (30–70 CE) might not have been too short a period for undue embellishment of the tradition to have occurred, and whether the original eye-witnesses might not have checked such embellishment. They have questioned whether the early church might not have had, among its other interests, a purely biographical or historical interest in Jesus. They have noted that the New Testament itself lays claim to the authenticity of the traditions it transmits (cf. e.g. 1 Cor. 15:1ff.; Lk. 1: 1ff.; Acts 1:21–22, 10:39–41; Jn 19:35, 21:24; 1 Jn 1:1–3; 1 Pet. 5:1; 2 Pet. 1:16), and pointed out that the rabbinic tradition took care to preserve the sayings of prominent rabbis, and hence, why not the early church those of Jesus. The framework of the gospel narrative, according to some scholars, was not wholly artificial but had a basis in tradition.[51] Critics have also highlighted the lack of consensus among form critics themselves as to the classification and *sitz im leben* of the forms. The forms are not all 'pure', and many are of mixed type (cf. Mk 2:3–12 or 3:1–6, for example, each of which could be described as a miracle story, but also as an apophthegm, or controversy dialogue, with polemic as its *sitz im leben*). The *sitz im leben* of a Gospel unit might not in itself be a reliable guide to history. The tendencies of oral tradition, too, are not fixed 'laws' and sometimes operate in reverse. Too creative a role in the formation of gospel tradition may be being assigned by form critics to the community, and not enough either to Jesus himself (level 1) or to the evangelists (level 3; see p. 42).

Some of these criticisms are pertinent, although form critics would respond by saying that their method, being an inferential one (i.e. it works back from the texts and deduces what must have happened to the Jesus tradition in the oral period), avoids the *a priori* historicizing assumptions often made by conservative critics. New Testament writers may lay claim to the authenticity of their traditions, but these remain claims, and still need to be tested. The authenticity of traditions (especially sayings) credited to famous rabbis cannot likewise be treated at face value, and so for that reason rabbinic tradition has increasingly been subjected to the same form-critical process and criteria as the New Testament Gospels. Modern research has for the most part served to confirm K. L. Schmidt's ground-breaking analysis on the framework of the Gospel tradition, and redaction criticism, which we shall shortly be considering, has not only corrected form criticism's one-sided emphasis on the creativity of the early church, but offered some explanation for the 'counter-tendencies' of the tradition as well as for the 'mixed' forms encountered in the Gospels, by attributing these to the editorial 'interference' of the evangelists.

What, then, are the assured results of form criticism? In the first place, form criticism has taught us that the Gospels are not biographical but *kerygmatic*. They were written 'out of faith for faith'. They present the church's view of Jesus, or that of the evangelists. They intend to win readers to that view. They proclaim the faith, and intend to produce faith. They intend to convert. They are *kerygmatic* or, to put it in more secular terms, they are religious propaganda.

Second, form criticism has made us aware that historical data about Jesus cannot be 'assumed' directly from the Gospels, but has to be 'gleaned' after careful application of critical method. Gospel tradition was transmitted orally, and not written directly from personal reminiscence. Hence, the historical Jesus of the primary tradition can only be approached through analyses of the tradition, first in the literary text, then in the oral tradition preceding the text, and finally by working back to the primary historical level.

Third, form criticism has drawn our attention to the fact that, in our analyses, due account must be taken of the role played by the practical needs of the community on the formation of the Gospel tradition. At each stage of transmission, the selection and shaping of the material was governed by these practical needs: worship (liturgy), parenesis, teaching, catechesis, discipline, preaching, polemic, apologetic.

Finally, in respect of the compilation of the Gospel tradition, form criticism has demonstrated to us that the arrangement of the material in our Gospels was 'determined', as R. H. Fuller points out, 'by topical and theological considerations rather than (except in the broadest outline) by the actual course of events'.[52] Some collections of like material were made prior to our Gospels but on the whole the actual arrangement of the pericopae can essentially be put down to the work of the evangelists.

Source criticism, the synoptic problem and the emergence of redaction criticism

The Gospels, then, were the product of a long, complex process of oral tradition culminating in written documents. The Gospel tradition had a history, in other words, and a complicated one. In chapter three, we noted the factors that led to the production of written documents, especially the Gospel literature, namely, the death of the first generation of believers, including the apostles, and the drying up of the oral tradition; the delay of the *parousia*, leading to a re-evaluation of Christianity, and especially of Jesus' message and teaching; the spread of Christianity into the Gentile world with a consequent impetus in the gathering of traditions about his words and deeds. In this chapter, we have seen that form criticism has advanced the view that the Gospels are not the direct historical transcripts of eye-witnesses but the compilation, the piecing together, the committing to writing by the later anonymous evangelists of the oral traditions of the communities to which they belonged, sayings and stories of Jesus which were circulating in these communities prior to their written composition. Having summarized form criticism's findings, it is now time to consider the second of our three critical methods, namely, source criticism.

The aim of source criticism is to determine whether certain units of oral tradition were brought together, and committed to writing, as seems the case, prior even to the composition of the Gospels as we have them before us. Did the evangelists themselves, in other words, use not only oral tradition but also written sources in their Gospels? While it is less certain in the case of Mark, this possibility is very strong in the case of Matthew and Luke, the prologue of whose Gospel reads:

> Inasmuch as many have undertaken to compile a narrative of the things which have been accomplished among us, just as they were delivered to us by those who from the beginning were eyewitnesses and ministers of the word, it seemed good to me also, having followed all things closely for some time past, to write an orderly account for you, most excellent Theophilus, that you may know the truth concerning the things of which you have been informed (Lk. 1:1).

But how do we determine if the evangelists have used not only oral tradition but written sources also in their Gospels? In general, the criteria pointing to the existence or use of sources, whether oral or written (as opposed to the evangelists' simply writing 'out of their heads' as it were) would be as follows.

The first criterion for the use of sources of any kind would be historical inconsistencies in the text under review, as revealed, for example, by the overlapping of content, the duplication of material, or what source critics call 'doublets'. Reference has already been made to the two feeding stories in the Gospel of Mark (Mk 6:34–44 = 8:1–9), but the following is an example from the Gospel of Matthew which seems to indicate that the evangelist had more than one source for the same tradition:

> As they were going away, behold, a dumb demoniac was brought to him. And when the demon had been cast out, the dumb man spoke; and the crowds marvelled, saying, 'Never was anything like this seen in Israel.' But the Pharisees said, 'He casts out demons by the prince of demons' (Mt. 9:32–34).

> Then a blind and dumb demoniac was brought to him, and he healed him, so that the dumb man spoke and saw. And all the people were amazed, and said, 'Can this be the Son of David?' But when the Pharisees heard it they said, 'It is only by Beelzebub, the prince of demons, that this man casts out demons' (Mt. 12:22–24).

A second criterion for the use of sources in general would be literary inconsistencies, for example, breaks, disruptions, dislocations, disjointedness in the sequence or flow of the evangelists' presentation. Source critics call these 'aporias'. A classic instance occurs at the end of John chapter 14, verse 31 where the Johannine Jesus ends a long discourse with the words:

> [B]ut I do as the Father has commanded me, so that the world may know that I love the Father. Rise, let us go hence.

Instead of rising with his disciples, however, and going hence, the Jesus of the Johannine text continues discoursing for another three long chapters, and it is only at the beginning of chapter 18, that the action expected by the reader is taken:

> When Jesus had spoken these words, he went forth with his disciples across the Kidron valley, where there was a garden, which he and his disciples entered (Jn 18:1).

Such aporias – which, in this Johannine case, suggests the inexpertly edited insertion of supplementary or extraneous material – are prominent throughout the Gospel of Mark. The 'Levi' called to be a follower of Jesus in chapter 2, verse 14 is curiously not mentioned in the disciples' list of chapter 3, verses 13–19. Throughout chapter 4, verses 1–34, the Markan Jesus delivers his parable discourse to the crowds from the consistent vantage-point of a boat, yet in verses 10–12, the location appears to be different. The disciples are later directed to Bethsaida by Jesus (6:45), but the boat mysteriously lands in Gennesaret (6:53). Stylistic inconsistencies, too – where, for example, one part or section of a text is written in a different literary style from another – are frequently met with in the Gospels. In the Gospel of Luke, in the birth and infancy narratives unique to the third evangelist (1–2), we encounter a Hebraic style (similar to that of the Old Testament) which is less apparent elsewhere in the Gospel, and which some scholars have seen as a pointer to the use of sources.

A third criterion for the use of sources, whether oral or written, would be theological inconsistencies (or inconsistencies in the ideas presented in general). In the examples below, of three separate sayings found on the lips of Jesus, all taken from the Gospel of Mark, one can detect perhaps three alternative stances towards the notion of an imminent eschaton. In the first, Jesus predicts the end-time specifically in the lifetime of his hearers; in the second, we are told that the end-time will not come, in effect, before the mission to the Gentiles; and in the third, no one knows, not even Jesus, when it will come:

> And he said to them, 'Truly, I say to you, there are some standing here who will not taste death before they see the kingdom of God come with power' (Mk 9:1).

> And the gospel must first be preached to all nations (Mk 13:10).

> But of that day or that hour no one knows, not even the angels in heaven, nor the Son, but only the Father (Mk 13:32).

The form critic can usually explain the historical, literary or theological inconsistencies within the Gospel texts in terms of the diverse units of oral tradition employed by the evangelists, some going back to the earliest levels or strata of the tradition, others reflecting later stages. In the case of the above examples, the first saying may be genuinely dominical (since the early church is unlikely to have invented a saying which was not, in fact, fulfilled), the second might emanate from a time after the early church's mission to the Gentiles, and the third possibly from the evangelist himself, i.e. from the period when there was real uncertainty over Jesus' return, and when the delay of the *parousia* necessitated revised thinking or new perspectives on eschatological matters. In these individual cases, however, there is no need to posit the use by the evangelists of written sources.

How, then, to return to our question, do we determine if the evangelists have used not only oral tradition but written sources also in their Gospels? Was there an interim stage between oral tradition and the compilation of the Gospels, a stage when oral material was incorporated into written sources prior to the Gospels? To prove this, i.e. to prove that discrepancies or aporias in the text may be more than the product of separate, discrete, diverse traditions, the source critic must show that the Gospels incorporate a larger, more extensive sequence of traditional material, a broader linkage of Gospel units (or pericopae). To prove the incorporation of written sources as opposed to oral traditions, he or she must show, moreover, that this more extensive sequence has its own characteristic language and style, its own vocabulary, its own positive and negative distinguishing features, its own distinctive ideas and theology – its own unity, in other words.

To show that any of our Gospels are dependent upon prior written documents, to show *literary* dependence, in other words, the source critic looks for extensive written agreement between that Gospel and whatever documentary source(s) it may be suspected of being based upon. The criteria for *literary* relationship are fourfold, namely, extensive agreement in terms of *content*, *form*, *order* and *wording*.

When these criteria for literary relationship are considered, a surprising observation emerges. This observation was made at least as early as Augustine in the fourth century CE but its significance was not critically examined until the eighteenth century. The fact emerges that on these grounds three of our four Gospels would seem to have a literary relationship *with each other*. One or more of these three Gospels has used one or more of the others as its source. It is the nature of this literary relationship that constitutes what scholars call the 'Synoptic Problem'.

These three Gospels are, of course, Matthew, Mark and Luke. The Fourth Gospel, the Gospel of John, is the 'odd man out'. We can see this when we observe the similarities existing between them vis-à-vis the Fourth Gospel in content, form, order and wording.

Where content is concerned, the number of pericopae shared by Matthew, Mark and Luke is extensive. Of Luke's 1,149 verses, only 580 verses are not found in the other two. Of Matthew's 1,068 verses, only 300 verses are not found in the other two. Of Mark's 661 verses, only 31 are not found in the other two. 630 of Mark's 661 verses, in other words, are also found in Matthew and Luke. The Fourth Gospel, on the other hand, has far less of this common material. It has only a few narratives or sayings in common, and where they do occur, they are often in different contexts: cf. e.g. the Cleansing of the Temple (Jn 2:13–22; cf. Mk 11:15–19 and par.), the Feeding of the Five Thousand and the Walking on the Water (Jn 6:1–15, 16–21; cf. Mk 6:34–44, 45–52 and par.), Peter's Confession (Jn 6:66–71; cf. Mk 8:27–33 and par.), the Entry into Jerusalem (Jn 12:12–19; cf. Mk 11:1–10 and par.) and several sections of the Passion Narrative (e.g. Jn 18:15–27; cf. Mk 14:53–72).

In respect of form, the same types of traditional material (pericopae) are found strung together in the same way in Matthew, Mark and Luke, in what form critics call a 'unit structure': apophthegms, wisdom sayings, apocalyptic and prophetic sayings, legal sayings and community rules, Christological sayings, parables, miracle stories. One can observe a series of parables, for example, in the parallel passages of Mark chapter 4, verses 1–34, Matthew chapter 13, verses 1–51 and Luke chapter 8, verses 4–18. One can also see a number of apophthegms, with a controversy theme, in Mark chapter 2, verses 1–22, Matthew chapter 9, verses 1–17 and Luke chapter 5, verses 17–39. These distinctive forms are pieced together or combined in the same basic way to produce a somewhat anecdotal presentation. Only the passion narrative, as we have seen, forms a larger connected narrative. In contrast, while it has a number of Christological sayings (indeed far more than Matthew, Mark or Luke), and a passion narrative, the Fourth Gospel contains on the whole far fewer, and in some cases even lacks many of these other types of material. It has no parables, for example, or exorcism stories. The overall presentation consists of larger discourse compositions often developing out of the preceding core narratives (cf. e.g. chapters 4, 5, 6, 9 and 11). The unit structure, therefore, is not as apparent.

In addition to having the same types of material (or forms), Matthew, Mark and Luke present their units (or pericopae) for the most part in roughly the same order. The sequence can be briefly summarized as the appearance of John the Baptist, Jesus' baptism, the temptation pericopae, the Galilean ministry culminating in Jesus' journey to Jerusalem, his appearance there, the Cleansing of the Temple, his confrontation with the authorities, his apocalyptic discourse, the arrest, trial, crucifixion and resurrection. By contrast, in the Fourth Gospel, Jesus' Cleansing of the Temple is recounted at the start of his ministry, not at the end. Jesus makes numerous visits to Jerusalem rather than one climactic one lasting approximately a week. There is a longer Judaean ministry (from Jn 7:10 onwards Jesus is found almost exclusively in Jerusalem and Judaea) as well as a Galilean one.

Matthew, Mark and Luke not only have common material, the same basic types or 'forms' of material, the same basic ordering of this material but also the same basic wording in many of the pericopae. You can see this, for example, if you compare (preferably with a synopsis), Mark 1:40–45 with Matthew 8:1–4 and Luke 5:12–16, or Mark 2:1–12 with Matthew 9:1–8 and Luke 5:17–26, or Mark 11:27–33 with Matthew 21:23–27 and Luke 20:1–8. In these common pericopae, Matthew has fifty-one percent of Mark's actual words, and Luke has fifty-three percent.

By virtue of common material, common form, common order and common wording, these three Gospels can be 'looked at' or 'seen together'. Hence, they are described as the 'Synoptic' Gospels (from the Greek meaning 'to see together'). A 'synopsis', as we have already seen, is a book which places the text of the three Gospels in parallel columns so that they may more easily be compared and contrasted, and B. H. Throckmorton's *Gospel Parallels* (1979) has been recommended. It is when the three Gospels are compared in this way, that the 'Synoptic Problem' emerges. When comparisons are made, the Synoptic Gospels are found not only to have striking similarities, but also to have striking differences.

In the first place, two of the three, i.e. Matthew and Luke, have a body of common material not shared by the third, Mark. This common material often shows striking verbal agreement (cf. e.g. Mt. 3:7b–10, 12 = Lk. 3:7b–9, 17). It consists of some 250 verses of Matthew's 1,068 verses and of Luke's 1,149 verses. In Matthew it is found in five main blocks or discourse sections, namely:

5–7	The Sermon on the Mount
10	The Mission Discourse
13	The Parable Discourse
18	The Discourse on the Church
23–25	The Denunciation of the Pharisees and the Apocalyptic Discourse

In Luke it is found in two main blocks only (and mixed with narrative material), namely:

6:20–8:3	The (so-called) Small Insertion
9:51–18:14	The (so-called) Large Insertion (or Travel Narrative)

This material, it is to be emphasized, is not found in Mark. Mark lacks, therefore, the Sermon on the Mount (or Plain, in Luke), has fewer parables, has no long discourse on the sending out of the twelve, and no long discourse on the woes against the Pharisees.

A second striking difference is that all three Gospels have special material not shared by the others. This consists of 31 verses of Mark's 660 verses, 300 verses of Matthew's 1,068 verses (i.e. almost one third), and 580 verses of Luke's 1,149 verses (i.e. almost one half). This material comprises, for example:

1. In Mark: 4:26–29 (the parable of the developing seed); 7:31–37 (the miracle story of the deaf and dumb man); 8:22–26 (the miracle story of the blind man); 14:52 (the story of the naked youth);
2. In Matthew: 1–2 (the birth narrative and genealogy); 5–7 (sections of the Sermon on the Mount); 28 (the post-resurrection appearances, esp. the Great Commission, 28:18–20);

3. In Luke: 1–2 (separate birth and infancy narratives with some irreconcilable differences with Matthew; there is no birth narrative in Mark); 15 (parables); 24 (separate post-resurrection appearances, again quite different from Matthew; Mark does not give any such appearances).

The 'Synoptic Problem', therefore, can be framed as follows: how can we explain the considerable, often striking similarity between these three Gospels, and at the same time the considerable, often striking differences between them? Is there a pattern to be observed in all this that might provide a clue to the unravelling of the Synoptic Problem? Scholars claim that there is, and it is to be discerned, first of all, by looking again at the content, order and wording of the passages which all three Gospels share in common (the so-called Triple Tradition).

Almost all of the content of Mark's Gospel is to be found in either of the other two Gospels. To remind ourselves, of Mark's 661 verses, Matthew has the equivalent of 606 (they are condensed to 500). He lacks 55 verses only. Of these 55 verses, Luke has 24. Hence, there are only 31 verses of Mark which don't appear in either of the other two.

Where differences in order occur, there is a pattern of *major agreement*. This pattern of major agreement is as follows: Matthew agrees with Mark's order where Luke differs from it; Luke agrees with Mark's order where Matthew differs from it, but Matthew and Luke seldom agree with one another in the ordering of material over against Mark. Mark, to put it another way, is almost never the 'odd man out'.

Where differences in wording occur in passages common to all three, the pattern of major agreement is the same. Matthew agrees with Mark over against Luke, Luke agrees with Mark over against Matthew, but Matthew and Luke seldom agree with one another against Mark. Mark again is seldom the 'odd man out'. *Minor* agreements, that is, agreements between

Matthew and Luke over against Mark in terms of wording (and less commonly order) do exist, it is fair to point out, but the pattern of *major* agreement is as above.

Mark represents, then, the common *denominator* with regard to all three. Four main solutions, as a result, can and have been posited with Mark as the common ground or significant factor in the equation (others have been suggested, but have not commanded any significant measure of support), and these are represented in Figure 1 below.

Solution 1. has never been a serious contender. It asks us to believe that a Gentile–Christian Gospel was first, and that the progressively more Jewish Gospels were written later and based on it. The author himself also lays claim to earlier accounts of the life of Jesus which predate his own (Lk. 1:1).

Solution 2. is the so-called Griesbach hypothesis. It is named after J. J. Griesbach who proposed it in 1789, and it has been vigorously restated in recent times by W. R. Farmer.[53] This theory claims that Mark is the latest of the Gospels and is essentially an extract or abridgment of both Matthew and Luke. The theory is supported, among other things, by the alleged evidence of conflation in Mark, i.e. the practice, when copying, of combining two or more alternative readings when unable to make a choice between them. The following is frequently cited as an example, the first showing Matthew's version of the passage,

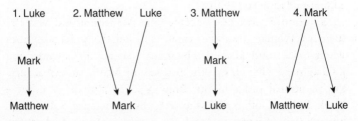

Figure 1 The Synoptic problem: some proposed solutions.

the second, Luke's, and the third that of Mark, who is deemed to be conflating his two earlier sources:

> *That evening,* they brought to him many who were *possessed with demons* (Mt. 8:16).

> Now *when the sun was setting,* all those who had *any that were sick* with various diseases brought them to him (Lk. 4:40).

> *That evening, at sundown,* they brought to him *all who were sick* or *possessed with demons* (Mk 1:32).

But what purpose would this abridgment of two Gospels have served? Why would Mark have omitted so much extraordinary material (e.g. the birth and infancy narratives, the Sermon on the Mount, many of the parables, the post-resurrection appearances)? Why, if abridgment were the purpose, are the Markan narratives generally much longer (cf. e.g. Mk 5:21–43 and par.)? Why did Mark *add* two miracle stories of dubious value (7:31–37; 8:22–26) to his abridged version of the other two Gospels, and omit sayings material of inestimable worth? As for the supposed conflation pattern in Mark, a number of scholars, following F. Neirynck, would prefer to see these as examples of Markan 'duality', of 'duplicate' or 'two-step expressions'. This is a consistent Markan stylistic feature whereby the evangelist is seen to make one statement immediately followed by another, the second adding precision to the first.

Solution 3. was first accepted by Augustine and was the standard Roman Catholic view until relatively recent times when it was stoutly defended by scholars such as B. C. Butler and J. Chapman.[54] It holds to the priority of Matthew, and accepts the traditional order in our New Testament texts: Matthew–Mark–Luke. It suffers from the same disadvantage as Solution 2., however, since it claims Mark as an abbreviation of Matthew.

It has the additional complication in that Luke must also have used Matthew, as well as Mark if we are to account for the material common to each but not shared by Mark. But then Luke would have had no need of Mark since his Markan material was already to a substantial degree to be found in Matthew, and if he did copy both, his editorial (or redactional) procedure requires some explanation!

Solution 4., the standard solution, is accepted by most scholars as the one giving rise to the fewest problems or difficulties. This claims that Mark's Gospel was prior, and that Matthew and Luke both independently copied it as a source.

The case for Markan priority can be supported with a number of arguments. There is, first, the argument from content. All but 31 verses of Mark are present in either Matthew or Luke. There is, secondly, the argument from order. Mark's order is almost always followed by either Matthew or Luke. Third, there is the argument from wording. Mark's wording is adopted, with few exceptions, by either Matthew or Luke, who seldom agree together against Mark. All of these phenomena are explicable, of course, although with some strain, by the other solutions advanced. Further arguments, however, have been adduced. There is, fourthly, the argument from primitiveness. The Greek of both Matthew and Luke is better than that of Mark. It is more likely, therefore, that Matthew and Luke improved Mark's Greek than that he adulterated theirs. Mark paints a harsher portrait of Jesus' disciples, as we shall see in chapter five, and his view of Jesus, although highly theological, is less sophisticated than that of the other two evangelists. It is more likely, therefore, that Matthew and Luke would have removed these features, or altered or developed Mark's theology than that he would have created a less reverential portrait out of theirs. Fifth, there is the argument from brevity. Mark's Gospel is shorter than the Gospels of Matthew and Luke. It is more likely, therefore, that the longer Gospels of Matthew and Luke would have enlarged the shorter Gospel of

Mark (perhaps because of its perceived deficiencies) by adding their own birth (and infancy) narratives, their supplementary parables and sayings material, and their separate post-resurrection appearance stories, than that Mark would have produced a shorter Gospel by omitting this significant material. In short, in the classic words of G. M. Styler, 'given Mk, it is easy to see why Matt, [we may also add Lk.] was written; given Matt, [or Lk.], it is hard to see why Mk was needed'.[55]

Markan priority offers a reasonable explanation, then, for one part of the 'Synoptic Problem', namely, that of the Triple Tradition and the interrelationship involved between Mark, Matthew and Luke in respect of their common material, but we still have the problem of the material that Matthew and Luke have in common but which Mark does not share, the so-called 'Double Tradition'. The majority of scholars believe that this common material was derived independently by Matthew and Luke from a common source, called Q (from the German *Quelle*, meaning a 'source'). Agreement at certain points in the exact wording and order suggests to some scholars that it was a written source. Others claim it was an oral one. Whatever form it took, it consisted mainly of 'sayings' material. Matthew and Luke have independently drawn upon two sources, therefore, Mark and Q, and hence this solution is called the Standard Two-Source theory, or the Two-Document hypothesis (2DH).

The process of reconstructing Q has gone on for some time now, and a number of questions have been addressed to it. When and where was it originally written, and in what language? How extensive a source was it, and does the common non-Markan material in Matthew and Luke define its extent? If it is to be considered a documentary source, can strata be distinguished within it, and did it develop in stages? If it is not merely a random collection of sayings, can we detect in it certain distinctive themes? Does it even have a theology distinguishable from that of the first and third evangelists who incorporated it?

What can be said, moreover, about the community from which it emanated, and whose concerns it originally addressed?

Answers are now emerging to these questions.[56] Scholars now think that it was composed between 40 and 70 CE in the area of Northern Galilee, and that it reflects the concerns and convictions of a community of conservative Jewish Christians with a continuing commitment to the covenant, the law and the Jerusalem Temple. This community had a strong eschatological emphasis which led them to expect the imminent kingdom of God and the return of Jesus as the apocalyptic Son of Man. What is lacking in its theology, when compared with that of Paul, for example, is any kind of soteriology which invests salvific significance in Jesus' death.

The Q hypothesis has been attacked by prominent scholars such as M. D. Goulder, and before him, A. Farrer.[57] Why can't Matthew and Luke be dependent on each other directly, the common material shared by them the result of direct borrowing, one from the other? The minor agreements between Matthew and Luke would also support this, since it is difficult to explain why, if both these evangelists were independently copying Mark, without knowledge of the other, there should be cases where their wording is identical, while Mark has something different or has not supplied it (cf. e.g. Mk 14:65, 'And some began to spit on him . . . and to strike him, saying to him, "Prophesy!"' with Mt. 26:67 '. . . saying, "Prophesy to us, you Christ! *Who is it who struck you*?"' and Lk. 22:63 '. . ."Prophesy! *Who is it that struck you*?"').

Those who defend the Q hypothesis point out that the Gospels of Matthew and Luke show no overall signs of mutual influence, whether literary or theological. Any mutual influence was exercised only in the later transmission of their texts, in the manuscript tradition, when copies were being made. The text of Luke, for example, was assimilated by scribes to that of Matthew to make them harmonize. If they were dependent on each other, then Luke's rearrangement of Matthew's material is incomprehensible, and vice versa. Matthew's material is organized into five discourse sections inserted at strategic points into the Markan framework (if we accept the standard solution). Would Luke have disrupted the orderly and skilful arrangement of Matthew's material in the way he would have needed to have done if we accept direct dependence? Why destroy the unity of Matthew's Sermon on the Mount (5–7) by omitting some material, or distributing other material to various places throughout the Lukan Gospel? The Matthean material (common to Matthew and Luke) is found in Luke's Gospel at virtually no point where Matthew had placed it in the (corresponding) Markan framework. Such precise 'filleting' of Matthew implies a knowledge of Mark and the implied procedure is a truly remarkable one! At no point does Luke take over any of the additions Matthew himself has made to the Markan text. Again, this implies an editorial (or redactional) policy that is difficult to fathom. Sometimes Matthew appears to have the more original form of a saying (e.g. Mt. 7:11, 'how much more will your Father who is in heaven give *good things* to those who ask him?'; cf. Lk. 11:13, 'how much more will the heavenly Father give the *Holy Spirit* to those who ask him?'), sometimes Luke (e.g. Lk. 6:20, 'Blessed are you poor, for yours is the kingdom of God'; cf. Mt. 5:3, 'Blessed are the poor *in spirit*, for theirs is the kingdom of heaven').

But what about the minor agreements between Matthew and Luke over against Mark? Although these continue to cast a question mark over the standard solution, most scholars are satisfied that a reasonable answer can be given. The minor agreements have been explained, for the most part, in three ways. First, as indicated above, by textual corruption, and especially as a result of scribes harmonizing Luke with Matthew. A second explanation would be that each may have been independently in possession of a superior tradition (perhaps an oral one) which led them to correct Mark. One example of this would be in Mark chapter 8, verse 31 and par., where the Markan text has Jesus predict his resurrection 'after three days' and both Matthew (16:21) and Luke

(9:22) concur in the wording 'on the third day'. Given the strong early Christian tradition that Jesus rose 'on the third day' in accordance with the scriptures (cf. e.g. 1 Cor. 15:4 and Hos. 6:2?), it is not difficult to see why Matthew and Luke may independently have emended Mark's version. This suggests, indeed, a third explanation for the minor agreements, namely, the application of a common but independent editorial (or redactional) policy. Both might have opted, with no knowledge of or reference to the other, to correct Mark's Greek, so ending up with the same or similar wording, or each may have decided to alter a theological emphasis in Mark with which they shared a common disagreement. We shall see examples of this in the next chapter when we consider the results of redaction criticism on the Gospels.

I have commented on the Triple Tradition (the material that all three evangelists have in common), and the Double Tradition (the material that only Matthew and Luke have in common). But all three Gospels also have material peculiar only to themselves. Scholars designate this material the Special Material, and, in the case of Matthew and Luke, where it is substantial, it is sometimes given the symbols M (Special Matthew) and L (Special Luke). There is no agreement, however, that this material constituted, in the case of each evangelist, a single, specific and unified *source* upon which they each drew. Special Matthew (M) and Special Luke (L) do not have the same status as Mark and Q, the two sources which are referred to in the Two-Source theory or the Two-Document hypothesis. Matthew's Special Material is disparate. It may be in part derived from oral tradition. Sometimes it may be Q material which Luke, on his part, has not included. At other times, it may be his own composition (as, for example, in 16:17–18). Likewise for Luke's Special Material. The origin and status of each passage so designated needs to be assessed on its own merits.

In earlier years, following B. H. Streeter,[58] when M and L were considered more unified sources, it was more usual to talk of the Four-Document hypothesis. Some scholars have even maintained that, since Special Luke consists largely of birth and infancy narratives, parables and a resurrection narrative, and is found always in connection with Q material, then the linkage may have been pre-Lukan. Q + L, in other words, were a primitive Gospel (proto-Luke) which Luke combined with Mark's Gospel. This interesting theory was suggested by B. H. Streeter himself, adopted by V. Taylor and others, but nowadays has no wide currency. Proto-Luke would be too fragmentary, it is generally agreed, to be a Gospel.

The standard solution to the Synoptic Problem nowadays, therefore, is that Matthew and Luke are the later Gospels, and that they each independently drew upon Mark and Q for their material, supplementing this with their own special material. This can be represented diagrammatically as shown below (Figure 2).

In consequence of this, the history of the Synoptic tradition can now be reconstructed. At the primary level of the tradition lie Jesus' own words and deeds, his teaching and activity, his life and death. Traditions about these words and deeds then circulated in the various Christian communities of the Mediterranean world after his death: first, in a Jewish and Palestinian milieu which

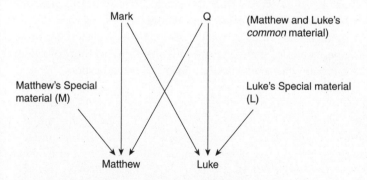

Figure 2 The standard solution to the Synoptic problem.

shaped and adapted them to the needs of these communities; second, in a Hellenistic–Jewish milieu as the Gospel spread outside Palestine, and third, in a Gentile milieu, especially after the Fall of Jerusalem. In each case, in this secondary stage of the tradition, the sayings and stories were coloured, shaped and moulded by the respective needs, activities and ideology of these different believing communities. Collections of like units were made, some possibly being written down for the first time, before the first Gospel texts were created. Q (the sayings source) seems to have been the earliest collection, and represents a Jewish–Palestinian tradition. Next came the compilation, from the oral tradition, of the Gospel of Mark, the first connected narrative of Jesus' life, and this marks the tertiary phase or level of the tradition. In turn, the later Gospels of Matthew and Luke were composed, using Mark and Q as their sources as well as the special material that derives from independent oral traditions or invention. Our ability to place the various sources behind the Synoptic Gospels into a clear framework of literary dependence and chronological sequence now makes possible a further development. If we can now determine what the source relationships are between the Gospels, then we can determine how each evangelist has treated the sources at his disposal. We can work out, in other words, what the evangelists owed to the tradition before them, and what they themselves embellished, altered, modified or invented. Source criticism paves the way for redaction criticism, therefore, and it is this third method of Gospel criticism which we shall examine in the next chapter.

5

Introduction to the Synoptic Gospels

Redaction criticism and the Gospel of Matthew

Thus far we have seen that a major fruit of a century and a half of New Testament scholarship has been the realization that the Gospels of Matthew, Mark and Luke are the product of a long and complex process of oral tradition culminating in the written texts that we now have before us. The evangelists were not eye-witnesses, in other words, of the events they purport to describe, nor are their Gospels accurate historical transcripts or precise biographical records of Jesus' life and death. The Synoptic evangelists used sources! The principal aim of Gospel source criticism, as we saw in chapter four, has been to determine what these sources were and to make some judgements about their historical reliability.

Nineteenth-century scholarship was preoccupied with source criticism, and important results were obtained, especially in the solution of the Synoptic Problem. To reiterate, in the case of Matthew and Luke, it was established, to the satisfaction of the majority of scholars, that Mark and a (hypothetical) sayings source Q were the main sources employed. Source criticism has been less successful in the case of the earliest Gospel Mark. In this case, no extensive written sources have as yet been isolated, although many attempts have been made. Nevertheless, in line with the standard solution to the Synoptic Problem, the source relations between the Gospels have now come to be summarized as presented in Figure 2 (p. 147). Moreover, with the Gospels placed, as a result, in temporal and dependent sequence, priority could now be given to Mark and Q as representing the earlier form (in the main) of the Jesus tradition, over against Matthew and Luke who represented the more developed form.

By the end of the nineteenth century, the earliest tradition about Jesus had therefore been taken back to Mark and to Q, but with Q remaining only a hypothetical source, and Mark (unlike Matthew and Luke) embodying, as we have said, no discernible written sources, Gospel scholarship appears to have been stymied. After the First World War, form criticism seemed to offer the answer. Behind the earliest Gospel, it declared, lay the oral tradition, and it was upon this oral tradition that Mark drew. Form criticism set itself the task, therefore, of tracing the Gospel tradition back into the oral phase. Its findings were examined in chapter four. The Gospels (especially Mark), it declared, are collections of separate, self-contained units of tradition, or *pericopae*, which circulated independently in various Christian communities. These individual units of tradition could be isolated and classified according to the shape or form they took in the oral tradition: apophthegms or pronouncement stories, wisdom sayings, prophetic or apocalyptic sayings, legal sayings or community rules, Christological sayings, parables, miracle stories, historical stories and legends in addition to a more extended passion narrative. Each *pericope* had its own setting or function (*sitz im leben*) in the early church, and its history of development in this oral phase could be traced (given a knowledge of the 'laws' or tendencies governing the transmission of oral tradition). Each was a product of the anonymous community, however, with form criticism (in company with its sister discipline source criticism) giving an insignificant role to the individual evangelist in its creation and/or transmission.

As one early, already mentioned, pioneer of the method, M. Dibelius, declared:

> The literary understanding of the synoptics begins with the recognition that they are collections of material. The composers are only to the smallest extent authors. They are principally collectors, vehicles of tradition, editors.[59]

These words illustrate again why the model of the Gospels for the form critics has been described as that of the pearl necklace. The pearls were important. The string was of very little worth!

This unbalanced picture was corrected, however, after the Second World War. From this period on, an increasing emphasis on the creative role played by the individual evangelists and the use made by them of their sources, either written or oral, has been a feature of Gospel studies. The Gospels are not merely scrapbooks or the evangelists mere 'scissors-and-pasters'! 'On the contrary', to cite the words of one redaction critic, 'the "scissors" were manipulated by a theological hand, and the "paste" was impregnated with a particular theology'.[60]

It was this awareness that led to the development of the new discipline, *Redaktionsgeschichte* ('redaction history') or redaction criticism. The term *Redactor* means 'editor' in German, but 'redaction' means more than editorial work. It means '*creative* editorial work', not mere editing in the sense of compiling or retouching older material but in the sense of subjecting it to creative transformation. Redaction criticism, or 'redaction history', is the study of the way the evangelists have handled their sources at the final stage of Gospel composition. It addresses questions such as 'How have they modified them, or (re)arranged them?' 'To what extent have they created new material altogether?' 'What is the history of the Jesus tradition at its final stage?'

How, then, can the aims of redaction criticism be summarized? In a word, redaction criticism focuses on the way an author or editor, in this case the evangelist, has 'adapted ("redacted") earlier materials to his own theological ends. . . . Redaction is the conscious reworking of older materials in such a way as to meet new needs.'[61] Where form criticism deals with the origin of the Gospel tradition, redaction criticism, as we have said, deals with it at a later stage, the final stage of Gospel composition. Where form criticism looks at the oral tradition in all its fragmentation, redaction criticism looks at the process of synthesis conducted by the individual evangelists on that tradition. In so doing, it seeks to determine the distinctive theological intention of the evangelists and their purpose in writing. It shades off into general literary criticism, therefore. Indeed there are times when the distinction between the evangelist as editor and the evangelist as author begins to look a little blurred! The virtue of redaction criticism, however, is that it views the individual Gospels as a whole, and not as a pastiche of fragments. Where the form critic looks at individual trees, in other words, the redaction critic looks at the contours of the wood itself, in relation to the landscape. Why is a particular tree planted where it is? Why are certain types of trees clustered where they are? What does this tell us about the art or design of the landscape gardener or forester?

Form criticism came to the fore after the First World War and was associated, as we have seen, with the names and work of three prominent German scholars, K. L. Schmidt, M. Dibelius, and R. Bultmann (as well as one British scholar, V. Taylor). Redaction criticism flowered after the Second World War and is likewise associated with the names of three influential German scholars, each of whom worked independently on the three Synoptic Gospels: G. Bornkamm on Matthew (Bornkamm was a pupil of Bultmann, and with G. Barth and H. J. Held wrote a book entitled *Tradition and Interpretation in Matthew*), H. Conzelmann on Luke and W. Marxsen on Mark.[62] These scholars, of course, had their precursors, W. Wrede (*The Messianic Secret in the Gospels*, 1901), for example, at the start of the century, or, between the wars, another German scholar, E. Lohmeyer, or the British scholar, R. H. Lightfoot (*History and Interpretation in the Gospels*, 1934),[63] but, in the post-war period, the method became more of a discipline under these three. Their common approach led to the coining by Marxsen of the term *Redaktionsgeschichte* for it.

All three scholars, it should be stressed, accepted the method and conclusions of form criticism. However, up until then the Gospel tradition was seen as having two settings only. Each saying or narrative had a possible setting in the life and teaching of the historical Jesus (what scholars, borrowing from archaeology, call the primary level, as we have already seen, or first stage, of the Gospel tradition), and a setting in the life of the early church (the secondary level or second stage of Gospel tradition). Marxsen's major contribution was to assert that each saying or narrative had potentially a third setting, namely, a setting in the Gospels, in the thought of each evangelist, and in the life situation of the particular community to which and for which he speaks. The writing of the Gospels was a unique event, in other words. At that point, the diverse and fragmented Jesus tradition, with all its varied sayings and stories about him, was brought together and synthesized. It was the evangelists, Marxsen insisted, and not the otherwise anonymous community, who were responsible for the selection of the material in our Gospels, and, to a significant degree, for its arrangement. Like the community before them, however, they too modified it, altered it, reshaped it, and (in some cases) expanded it. In each case, the individual evangelists have interpreted and sometimes reinterpreted the tradition they have received. Redaction criticism seeks to determine how this has been done and to what extent. In short, it seeks to determine the unique or distinctive contribution that the evangelists have made to the already developing tradition about the founder of Christianity.

How, then, do redaction critics go about their work? In general the first step is the same as that for form and source criticism, namely, the separation of traditional material from editorial material, of source from redaction. The source material, as we have said, may be written or oral. If written, it is investigated by the source critics. If oral, it is investigated by the form critics. Redaction critics, concentrate, however, on the redaction – or the 'string', the 'paste', the 'framework', the 'stitching', the 'matrix', whatever you may like to call it!

What in particular is the redaction critic looking for? Where can he or she hone in on the evangelist's contribution? At what points in a Gospel text is the editor's own hand most apparent? What, to put it another way, is 'grist' for the redaction critic's 'mill'? The following is a list of items which might appear on a redaction critic's list: the evangelist's selection, (re)arrangement and internal modification of the source material; the significant additions to, expansions of, and insertions into these sources; the introduction or conclusion to the Gospel where the evangelist has often given himself a freer rein; the 'seams' connecting the individual units (a term drawn from needlework), the transitional passages linking sections of the narrative, or the summaries outlining what comes before and after; the distinctive vocabulary or ideas vis-à-vis the source(s), especially as they appear in the editorial passages; the settings in which the sayings or stories appear, especially if they differ from the source (and may thereby have given the saying or story a new meaning); the evangelist's Christology, or estimate of the person of Jesus, especially as this is revealed in the use of Christological titles.

Where the sources are known, as with Matthew or Luke, the redaction-critical method can produce reasonably reliable, some have even claimed scientific, results. Mark was a source for both, and we have Mark before us. Q was a second source for both, and using critical methods, scholars have gone a long way to reconstructing the original version(s) of Q. Comparison, using the redaction–critical method, can then determine the nature and significance of the Matthean or Lukan redactional work on these sources.

Let us now turn to Matthew's Gospel, therefore, and apply the redaction–critical method to it. In this chapter, I shall only be concerned with what can be gleaned about the Gospel using this method. For a more general introduction to Matthew, you must consult the standard introductions and commentaries listed in the Further Reading section at the end. Moreover, I shall concentrate on what Matthew has done with Mark only (and not therefore with Q), and shall limit myself to four redactional areas: modifications, rearrangements, insertions and expansions. First of all, I will describe what you would observe when comparing the passages in Matthew with those in his Markan source, and then I will comment on the overall significance of these observations.

The modifications made by Matthew to Mark's text are of two major kinds: stylistic (or literary) modifications and theological modifications. Where style is concerned, a major observation is that Matthew has improved Mark's Greek. Indeed, it was his superior literary style, you recall, which was one of the factors arguing in favour of Markan rather than Matthean priority.

Where theology is concerned, two observations can be made. In the first place, Matthew offers his readers a more reverential portrayal of Jesus. In comparison with Mark's account, one notes how the Matthean evangelist often heightens Jesus' miraculous powers. In Matthew (8:13, 9:22, 15:28 and 17:18 and par.), the Matthean Jesus' cures occur *instantly* or *from that very hour*, we are told. In Matthew chapter 8, verse 16, 'he cast out the spirits *with a word*', says the evangelist. In Matthew chapter 12, verse 15 (and par.) where Mark has Jesus cure *many*, Matthew has him cure *all*. In Matthew (8:28ff. and 20:30), where Mark has Jesus cure one individual, Matthew has him cure *two*! In Matthew (4:23 and 9:35), using a characteristic Matthean formula, the evangelist describes Jesus as 'healing every disease and every infirmity'. One notes, too, Matthew's omission of the more dubious miracle stories of Mark (7:31–37 and 8:22–26). Here, the Markan Jesus is seen to labour over his cures. Some have even suggested that the duplication by Matthew of the individuals in chapter 8, verse 28 and chapter 20, verse 30 might have been conceived by way of compensation for these omissions! Matthew also alters Mark's miracle stories into (much abbreviated) illustrative didactic stories which are retold for the edification of the church. These stories are important for the message they convey about Jesus to Matthew's readers, and not for their details. They illustrate the nature and role of faith and discipleship, and often culminate, as a result, in a saying to that effect (cf. e.g. Mt. 9:27–31 and par.; 15:21–28 and par.). In form-critical terms, Matthew can be seen transforming the Markan miracle stories into apophthegms (paradigms or pronouncement stories).

In the second place, Matthew offers his readers a more reverential portrayal of Jesus' original disciples. One notes, for example, that where they are uncomprehending in Mark's Gospel (e.g. Mk 6:52), they clearly understand Jesus' words according to Matthew (cf. 13:16–17, 51, 16:12, 17:13 and par.). Where they fail to recognize who Jesus is in Mark, they recognize and confess Jesus as Son of God in the corresponding passages in Matthew (cf. 14:31–33, 16:16b–18 and par.). Where their role in Mark appears to be limited to being with Jesus, preaching and exorcising demons (cf. Mk 3:13–14) and bearing testimony (cf. Mk 13:9), they are given a more prominent role to play in Matthew, especially in the post-Easter church (cf. 10, 19:28, 28:18–20 and par.). If you want to check this out, have a look at the following Markan passages, and then compare these (preferably using a synopsis) with the corresponding Matthean ones to see what modifications have been introduced (Mk 6:52 and Mt. 14:33; Mk 9:33–34 and Mt. 18:1; Mk 10:35 and Mt. 20:20).

Where rearrangements are concerned, Matthew follows Mark's order for the most part but one prominent exception is that he combines the miracle stories found in Mark chapters 1, 2, 4–5 and 10 into a single (and perhaps significant) block of ten in 8–9. We will come back to this observation when considering the overall significance of Matthew's redactional activity.

Matthew's insertions are of two main types, sayings material and quotations from the Old Testament (or Hebrew Bible). As previously noted, he inserts five blocks of sayings or discourse material into the Markan framework. To remind you, these five blocks are as follows:

5–7	The Sermon on the Mount
10	The Mission Discourse
13	The Parable Discourse
18	The Discourse on the Church
23–25	The Denunciation of the Pharisees and the Apocalyptic Discourse

This inserted sayings material either comes from Q, or is Special Matthew (M) material (and hence may in part be his own creation). This can be seen particularly in the first of the five discourses, the famous Sermon on the Mount, which precedes the two miracle chapters of 8 and 9, and is so-called because it takes place on a mountain (Luke's parallel discourse takes place on a plain). The second, the Mission Discourse (or the Missionary Charge or Discourse to the Disciples), is an expansion of Mark chapter 6, verses 7–13. The third, the Parable Discourse (or the Parables of the Kingdom), comes from Mark chapter 4, verses 1–34 but is expanded with Q or M material. The fourth, the Discourse on the Church, is concerned with church discipline and has some basis in Mark chapter 9, verses 42–50. The fifth, the Denunciation of the Pharisees and the Apocalyptic (or Eschatological) Discourse, is a double discourse, the second part based on Mark chapter 13 but expanded with Q and M material (especially parables). Each discourse culminates in an almost identical formula which marks it off from the surrounding material: 7:28 ('And when

Jesus finished these sayings, the crowds were astonished at his teaching'); 11:1 ('And when Jesus had finished instructing his twelve disciples, he went on from there . . .'); 13:53 ('And when Jesus had finished these parables, he went away from there'); 19:1 ('Now when Jesus had finished these sayings, he went away from Galilee . . .'); 26:1 ('When Jesus had finished all these sayings, he said to his disciples . . .').

The second category of insertions is quotations from the Old Testament (or Hebrew Bible). Matthew has over sixty of these, the majority of which are not found in his Markan source. One special group are the so-called 'formula quotations'. These are prefaced with a characteristic formula, '[t]his took place in order to fulfil what was said by the prophets' or something similar (cf. e.g. 1:22–23, 2:5–6, 2:15, 2:17–18, 3:3, 4:14–16, 8:17, 12:17–21, 13:14–15, 13:35, 21:4–5, 26:56, 27:9–10). The purpose of these quotations is to prove that the events surrounding Jesus' life and death were the fulfilment of Old Testament prophecies. The evangelist, however, frequently distorts the Hebrew Bible to fit the event (e.g. 2:15, 'Out of Egypt have I called my son', Hos. 11:1, which refers to Israel and not the Christ child), or distorts his tradition or source to fit the Old Testament (e.g. 21:4–5 which, as previously noted, introduces *two* animals into Mark's story of Jesus' triumphal entry on the basis of Zech. 9:9). In some cases, the Old Testament may have furnished him with the details to create or embellish a tradition (cf. e.g. 26:15, 27:3–10, Judas and the thirty pieces of silver, with Zech. 11:12–13; Jer. 18:2ff., 32:6ff.; and Acts 1:16–20). Embellishing the Hebrew Bible text, or creating stories out of it, was a common practice in the Jewish circles of Matthew's day. In some cases, certain techniques of scriptural exegesis (e.g. midrash) led to such an imaginative embellishment of the Old Testament tradition that whole new incidents or stories were created out of it. Matthew may have followed this practice (cf. e.g. his birth stories, 1–2, or the story of Peter's walking on the water in 14:28–33 and par.).

Finally, there are Matthew's expansions of the Markan text to consider. Matthew not only expands his Gospel of Mark source within, but also at opposite ends. At one end, he attaches an account of Jesus' birth (1–2) where Mark had none (Mark begins with Jesus' baptism by John). This birth narrative comprises five components: a genealogy claiming Jesus as a descendant of King David through his father Joseph (although curiously Joseph is not stated to be his father!); Jesus' birth in David's city, Bethlehem; the visit of the Magi; the massacre of the innocents by Herod; the holy family's journey to Egypt and their return. At the opposite end (chapter 28), Matthew attaches post-resurrection appearances of Jesus to his disciples which are also absent from the Markan text. These are set in Galilee. They include a commission by Jesus to his disciples to go into all the world to spread his message, and, like the Sermon, they, too, are set on a mountain.

So much for what you would see if you made the above comparisons between the text of Matthew and his source Mark. These observations on the nature of Matthew's redaction have led to the recognition that Matthew's presentation or reinterpretation of his traditional material (Mark and Q) was influenced by four main things, namely, his understanding of the person of Jesus, his attitude to the role of the Jewish Law in relation to salvation, his position with regard to the church, and his stance with respect to the end-time: in other words, it was governed by his Christology, his soteriology, his ecclesiology and his eschatology.[64]

Where Christology is concerned, there are four things that can be said. First, Matthew follows Mark in emphasizing that Jesus was the 'Son of God', but where such a confession never appears on the lips of Jesus' disciples in Mark, Matthew places it on Peter's lips in Matthew chapter 16, verse 16 (= Mk 8:29) and in a Special Matthew passage which follows has Jesus commend Peter for the revelation he has received:

> Blessed are you, Simon Bar-Jonah! For flesh and blood has not revealed this to you, but my Father who is in heaven. And I tell

you, you are Peter, and on this rock I will build my church, and the powers of death shall not prevail against it (Mt. 16:17–18).

Second, Matthew seems to oppose Mark (cf. Mk 12:35–37) in emphasizing, on his part, that Jesus was the Jewish Messiah, the Son of David. He thus reveals the strongly Jewish–Christian nature of his Christology. Matthew's Gospel begins with a genealogy which seeks to prove that Jesus descended from King David, and has Jesus born in Bethlehem, the city of David. Jesus' putative father, Joseph, is addressed in a dream as 'son of David' by the angel, and Joseph's 'divine' son is in turn greeted in a similar fashion by the blind men (9:27, 20:30, 31) and the Canaanite woman (15:22). While the people initially wonder if he is the Son of David (12:23), the Jerusalem crowds and the children in the Temple proclaim him confidently as such (21:9, 15–16).

Third, Matthew introduces the idea that Jesus is the Suffering Servant of Isaiah. He makes this significant connection by means of two of the celebrated formula quotations which he adds to the Markan text:

That evening they brought to him many who were possessed with demons; and he cast out the spirits with a word, and healed all who were sick. This was to fulfil what was spoken by the prophet Isaiah, 'He took our infirmities and bore our diseases' (Mt. 8:16–17; cf. Isa. 53:4).

Jesus, aware to this, withdrew from there. And many followed him, and he healed them all, and ordered them not to make him known. This was to fulfil what was spoken by the prophet Isaiah: 'Behold, my servant whom I have chosen, my beloved with whom my soul is well pleased. I will put my Spirit upon him, and he shall proclaim justice to the Gentiles. He will not wrangle or cry aloud, nor will any one hear his voice in the streets; he will not break a bruised reed or quench a smoldering wick, till he brings justice to victory; and in his name will the Gentiles hope' (Mt. 12:15–21; cf. Isa. 42:1–4).

Fourth, Matthew presents Jesus throughout as the New Moses. The birth narrative is replete with echoes or resonances of the Moses story (e.g. the massacre of the innocents by Herod which calls to mind the slaying of the firstborn by Pharaoh; the holy family's sojourn in Egypt and their subsequent journey to Israel which recapitulates the theme of the exodus). Like Moses, and the people of Israel, Jesus spends a period in the wilderness (4:1–2). Following in the footsteps of Moses, he is a law-giver, indeed one not afraid to cite the law given by Moses, and to make it even more rigorous (5:17–20, 21–22, 27–28, 31–32, etc.). The five clearly demarcated blocks of teaching material inserted into the Markan framework by Matthew may be intended to mirror the five books of Moses, the so-called Pentateuch (Genesis, Exodus, Leviticus, Numbers, Deuteronomy), and it may not be too fanciful to see a hint of this already in the opening words of the Gospel: 'The book of the *genesis* [translated 'genealogy'] of Jesus Christ, the son of David, the son of Abraham' (1:1). Echoing the Sinai story, the first of these five discourses is set on a mountain (5:1). Like Moses, too, Jesus has an encounter with God on a mountain in which he is transfigured (17:1–8; cf. Exod. 20:20ff., 34:29–30). Following the first discourse are the two chapters (8–9) devoted by Matthew largely to miracles, and these perhaps reflect a second traditional image of Moses, namely, that of miracle-worker. Not surprisingly, therefore, the Matthean Jesus is shown exercising power over the elements (8:23–27; cf. the parting of the Red Sea in Exod. 14), or later supplying bread in the wilderness (14:13–21, 15:32–39; cf. Exod. 16). As with Moses, the Matthean Jesus' departing commission to his disciples also takes place on a mountain (28:16–20; cf. Deut. 31–34 and Moses' final departure from Mount Nebo before his followers enter the promised land).

With regard to Matthew's soteriology, a significant feature of his redaction is the attitude he reveals to the Jewish Law, and how he understands that Law in relation to the believer's salvation. If Jesus is seen as a New Moses, then he is also seen as bringing a new law. 'New' is perhaps not an entirely appropriate word, for Matthew sees Jesus as having called his disciples to a more stringent application of the Mosaic Law. Indeed, from those who would be saved (or who would 'enter the kingdom of heaven') the Matthean Jesus calls for a greater obedience to the spiritual principles embodied in the Mosaic law than even the Pharisees require. This comes out in his Special material:

> Think not that I have come to abolish the law and the prophets; I have come not to abolish them but to fulfil them. For truly, I say to you, till heaven and earth pass away, not an iota, not a dot, will pass from the law until all is accomplished. Whoever then relaxes one of the least of these commandments and teaches men so, shall be called least in the kingdom of heaven; but he who does them and teaches them shall be called great in the kingdom of heaven. For I tell you, unless your righteousness exceeds that of the scribes and Pharisees, you will never enter the kingdom of heaven (Mt. 5:17–20).

> The scribes and the Pharisees sit on Moses' seat; so practice and observe whatever they tell you, but not what they do; for they preach, but do not practice (Mt. 23:1–2).

Matthew's attitude to the law can be contrasted, therefore, with that of Paul, or even with that of Mark (cf. Mk 7:1–23, where the Markan Jesus exhibits what Jews would consider a lax attitude to the purity laws). Matthew's Jesus is also more unsympathetic to the Gentiles, as these strongly worded sayings indicate:

> Do not give dogs what is holy; and do not throw your pearls before swine, lest they trample them underfoot and turn to attack you (Mt. 7:6).

Go nowhere among the Gentiles, and enter no town of the Samaritans, but go rather to the lost sheep of the house of Israel . . . for truly you will not have gone through all the towns of Israel before the Son of Man comes (Mt. 10:5–6, 23).

I was sent only to the lost sheep of the house of Israel (Mt. 15:24).

If he [your erring brother] refuses to listen to them [one or two other church members] let him be to you as a Gentile and a tax collector (Mt. 18:17).

Matthew has accepted the inclusion of Gentiles within the church but, as with his fellow Jewish Christians, he appears to do so with a note of reluctance, and with an emphasis that the Jewish Law must still be kept by the followers of Jesus. This is borne out by his seeming interpretation of the Parable of the Wedding Feast (Mt. 22:1–10), and, in particular, by the puzzling addition he makes to it. In the main part of the story, those unworthy to share in the wedding feast (his fellow Jews?) are punished (with death and the burning of their city!), and the invitation of the king (God) is extended instead to whoever may be brought in to replace them from the streets (the Gentiles?). Having told a story which appears to demonstrate God's acceptance of non-Jews, the addendum of 22:11–14, nevertheless, has the king vent his anger on the individual who omits to wear a wedding garment (the requirements of the law?) and instructs his attendants to 'Bind him hand and foot, and cast him into the outer darkness; there men will weep and gnash their teeth' (22:13).

With respect to ecclesiology, Matthew views his community as the 'true Israel', exceeding the righteousness of the scribes and Pharisees in its obedience to the law brought by Jesus, the New Moses (5:20). His disciples are commissioned, therefore (in another Special Matthew passage), to go out into the world to teach people to observe this law (cf. 28:18–20, 'Go therefore and make disciples of all nations . . . *teaching* them to *observe* all that I have *commanded* you'). Matthew's is the most ecclesiastical of all the Gospels. As was mentioned in chapter 2, the word *ekklesia* (church) appears in the Gospel tradition only twice on Jesus' lips, and in each case it is in a Special Matthew passage (16:18, 18:17). This 'church', according to Matthew, was founded in Jesus' lifetime when Peter confessed Jesus not only as the Jewish Messiah, the Christ, but also as the 'Son of the living God', and was given authority to lead it as a result (16:16–20). In chapter 18, further Special Matthew material offers the Matthean reader the 'community rules' for the governance of this church.

Finally, in relation to eschatology, it is to be observed that Matthew once again stands closer to Jewish Christianity than the other Gospels. Hence, his eschatological emphases and stress on the coming end-time is stronger than in Mark and Luke. Matthew found this emphasis in Mark but adds to it. He inserts into the Markan framework additional apocalyptic material (cf. e.g. the eschatological parables in Matthew 25 which build on Mark's apocalyptic discourse). Consonant with what we have seen up until now, one strong element in this additional material (whether Q or M), is that when Jesus returns as Son of Man there will be a judgement. The Matthean Jesus will pronounce or execute judgement on those who have not kept his new law or commandments. One can see this in the Special Matthew parables of the Wheat and the Tares (13:24–30) or the Sheep and the Goats (25:31–46). These emphasize this final judgement. One can detect it also in the modifications which Matthew makes to the words of the Markan Jesus, as, for example, when he says of the apocalyptic Son of Man (Mk 8:38) not only that he will come 'in the glory of his Father with the holy angels', but also that 'he will repay every man for what he has done' (Mt. 16:27b). In Matthew's more concrete and dramatic version of the apocalyptic discourse, at the end-time itself 'there will appear the sign of the Son of man in heaven, and then all the tribes of the earth will mourn'

(Mt. 24:30; cf. Mk 13:26), and in his version of the Q parable added to that discourse (the Faithful and Wise Servant, Mt. 24:45–51 = Lk. 12:42–46), when the wicked servant is sent to the place of punishment, 'there men will weep and gnash their teeth' (24:51).

Redaction criticism and the Gospel of Luke

In the last section, I discussed the aims and methods of redaction criticism, and followed this up by seeing what could be said about the Gospel of Matthew, in particular its theology, in light of the third of our critical methods. Let us now turn to Luke and see what happens when we apply redaction criticism to the third Gospel. First, I intend to describe the nature of Luke's redaction, i.e. what you yourself would observe if you compared the text of Luke with that of his sources. For convenience, we shall again only focus on what Luke has done with his Markan source. As before, you may wish to examine the examples I give with the aid of a Gospel synopsis. For sake of brevity, we shall limit ourselves to describing Luke's redactional work in respect of five areas: his expansions, insertions, omissions, rearrangements and modifications of Mark. After this, we shall reflect on the significance of Luke's redaction in light of these changes. All of this is a bit like detective work, and so as I present my observations, you may wish to consider how you yourself would explain them.

The first thing to note is that Luke (as with Matthew) has expanded the Markan text both at the beginning and at the end. At the beginning, he provides the reader with a birth and infancy narrative (chapters 1 and 2) which is substantially different from that in Matthew. Luke's narrative begins in the Jerusalem Temple with an angelic prediction of John the Baptist's birth and future role. It comprises a visit by an angel to Mary also predicting

Jesus' birth and future role (note, by contrast, that all divine communications in Matthew's accounts are to Joseph, and via dreams). Although Luke may intend to date Jesus' birth at the same time as that reported by Matthew (the first evangelist giving his birth as during the reign of Herod the Great, who died in 4 BCE; cf. Mt. 2:1 and Lk. 1:5, 26), Jesus' actual birth is said to have occurred at the census under Quirinius, some ten years after the death of Herod the Great, on the deposition of his son Archelaus in 6 CE (cf. Lk. 2:1ff.). It also comprises a visit by shepherds, the purification of Mary and Jesus in the Temple, and a boyhood incident of Jesus precociously conversing with doctors of the law in the Temple: all stories which are absent in Matthew's account. At the end of his Gospel, Luke, in addition, presents us with post-resurrection appearances (ch. 24) absent in Mark. These, too, are different from the ones which Matthew also added to the end of the second Gospel. Luke's appearances, by contrast, are set in Jerusalem (not Galilee), and Jesus makes his departure at Bethany, the disciples returning to Jerusalem with express instructions not to leave the city (Lk. 24:49).

As with Matthew, Luke inserted sayings material into the Markan framework, but unlike the first evangelist did so in two main blocks (as opposed to Matthew's five discourse sections): 6:20–8:3 (the so-called 'small insertion') and 9:51–18:14 (the so-called 'large insertion'). These insertions comprise both Q and Special Luke material and are interspersed with narrative (in Matthew, sayings and narrative tend to be separate). Much of it is in the form of parables, again drawn from Q or representing material special to Luke, with most of these appearing in the large insertion.

As well as insertions, Luke has omitted material from his Markan source, a major example being the section in Mark from chapter 6, verse 45 to chapter 8, verse 26 (the so-called 'great omission'). Why Luke should have omitted so much Markan material here is not altogether clear, but one reason may have been to make way for his insertions and/or to avoid the duplicated material within his Markan source at this point (e.g. the second feeding story of Mk 8:1–10; cf. 6:30–44).

Certain curious rearrangements have taken place of the order Mark adopted for the pericopae in his Gospel. While following the Markan sequence for the most part, the third evangelist, for example, relates John the Baptist's arrest by Herod (related in Mk 6:14–29) *before* Jesus' baptism (see Lk. 3:18–20, 21–22). He also transfers Jesus' visit to his home town in Mark chapter 6, verses 1–6 to the beginning of his ministry (see Lk. 4:14–30), reproducing it in an expanded version, and placing it immediately *after* the temptation pericope (found in its brief Markan form in 1:12–13 and in its longer Q form in Mt. 4:1–11). At the same time, he presents the temptations of the Q version in a different order from those of Matthew so that Jesus' third and *final* temptation before he begins his ministry takes place in the Jerusalem Temple (see Lk. 4:9–11 and contrast Mt. 4:5–6 where the temptation in the Temple is the *second* of the three), after which the devil 'departed from him for an opportune time' (4:13).

A series of modifications to the Markan text can also be observed. Luke makes a number of literary alterations (the improvement of Mark's Greek, for example), and introduces a number of theological changes. Of particular interest are the embellishments he makes on a number of occasions. We have already noted that he has expanded Mark chapter 6, verses 1–6 into a speech by Jesus in his home synagogue (4:14–30), but he also presents Mark chapter 1, verses 16–20 as a miracle story (5:1–11), puts speeches into the mouths of the otherwise unde-fined robbers of Mark chapter 15, verses 27 and 32 (see Lk. 23:39–43) and, above all, qualifies Mark's harsh treatment of the disciples throughout. This he does, for example, by omitting (at 9:22) Jesus' harsh words to Peter in Mark chapter 8, verses 32–33, by promising Peter's rehabilitation after his denial (see Lk. 22:31–32 – another insertion!) and by abbreviating the

Gethsemane scene emphasizing the disciples' inability to keep watch with Jesus (cf. Mk 14:32–42 with Lk. 22:39–46, esp. v.45 where Luke's more sympathetic version reads '[Jesus] found them sleeping *for sorrow*').

In addition, Luke tends to qualify the imminent kingdom of God or *parousia* expectation of his source. He omits Mark chapter 1, verses 14–15, for example, where Mark has Jesus declare that 'the time is fulfilled and the Kingdom of God is at hand', and introduces a number of changes into the 'apocalyptic discourse' of Mark chapter 13 which warn the reader not to expect Jesus' return or the end of the world *at once* (cf. e.g. Lk. 21:8, 9 and par.). Where the Markan Jesus predicts that the High Priest and other members of the Jewish council or Sanhedrin 'will see the Son of Man seated at the right hand of Power, *and coming with the clouds of heaven*' (Mk 14:62), the Lukan version drops the final phrase and reads, 'From now on the Son of Man shall be seated at the right hand of the power of God' (Lk. 22:69), thereby orienting the words away from Jesus' future apocalyptic return to his present transcendent role.

A final example can be found in his treatment of the resurrection narratives. Luke places the resurrection appearances, as we have observed, in the vicinity of the more theologically significant Jerusalem rather than in Galilee (see Lk. 24:13–53) where Matthew (cf. Mt. 28:16–20), following a hint in Mark (see Mk 14:28, 16:7) had placed them. You may wish to look up Mark chapter 14, verse 28 and chapter 16, verse 7 for yourself, and their parallels in Luke, to see what Luke did with the words 'He is going before you to Galilee. *There* you will see him'! Luke also presents the resurrected Jesus as explaining to his disciples that his passion was the fulfilment of Old Testament scripture, promising them the Holy Spirit and predicting a Gentile mission beginning from Jerusalem (see Lk. 24:25–27, 49–53; Acts 1:1–11), where, at the finale, they are found 'continually in the temple blessing God'.

What, then is, the significance of these changes? And what has the redaction critic to make of the alterations introduced by Luke into his sources? The major work on Lukan redaction was done by H. Conzelmann who published his results in 1954 in a book called *Die Mitte der Zeit*. This means 'The Middle of Time' in German, but when translated into English, the book appeared with the more mundane title, *The Theology of St Luke*. While Conzelmann's work has been subsequently modified, and in some cases challenged, his pioneering redaction–critical analysis exposed the extent to which Luke was theologically motivated. The Gospel of Luke was composed somewhere around 75–100 CE in a Gentile setting, and has a distinctly pro-Gentile feel to it (in contrast to Matthew's Gospel which, as we have seen, has a Jewish flavour). For Luke's community, Conzelmann argued, the delay of the *parousia* was a major problem. Although he is not entirely consistent, Luke has addressed this problem by altering or modifying the earlier more imminent expectation of his sources. Hence, a claim that 'the time is at hand' is not to be heeded (Lk. 21:8), and the end will not be 'at once' (cf. Lk. 21:9). The interim period, in which his readers were now living, is in addition given theological status. It is the period of the church's mission to which Luke devotes the second volume of his major two-volume work, Luke–Acts. This period also begins, as the Gospel did, in and from Jerusalem (and its Temple) and recounts the systematic, indeed inexorable, spread of Christianity from the Holy City, the centre of the Jewish religious world, to Rome, the centre of the imperial world (cf. Acts 1:8).

Conzelmann asserted that what the third evangelist was essentially doing, therefore, was transmuting eschatology (belief about the imminent end of the world) into salvation history (belief about the continuous saving action of God in history). The earlier tradition found in Mark, with its more apocalyptic emphasis, has been reinterpreted by placing it within a much broader timescale. Conzelmann saw in the Gospel signs that the author envisaged three distinct periods or dispensations of salvation history: *the time of Israel* ('the law and the prophets') before Jesus (cf. e.g. 3:23–38, 16:16, 24:13–27, 44–49); *the sacred time of Jesus* (from baptism to ascension; cf. e.g. Acts 1:21–22, 10:36–43, esp. vv.37, 38); *the time of the Church* or *Holy Spirit* (cf. e.g. Acts 1:6–9). Luke's (Gentile) readers have therefore been made to reflect on the past, in which the Jewish scriptures (the Old Testament), the Messianic prophecies and the prophets up until John the Baptist all were seen as a preparation for the coming of Jesus (cf. Lk. 16:16, 24:27, 44). They have been made to consider in turn the sacred time when Jesus lived (the 'middle time' or *Mitte der Zeit* of Conzelmann's original title) in which the devil was temporarily routed (hence Lk. 4:13 and the later omission of Mk 8:33!), a period marked off from other periods, though now also past (cf. Acts 1:21–22, 10:37–38). They have also been alerted to the present time, the time of the church, and its historic mission to the world, with the *parousia*, as a result, an anticipated event in a less imminent future. Luke, Conzelmann claimed, had modified and rearranged his source material so as to produce, or reflect, this theologically motivated, threefold salvation history scheme.

And that is how some of his subtler changes are to be explained: the placing of John the Baptist's arrest (3:18–20) *before* Jesus' baptism (hence marking out John the Baptist as belonging to 'the time of Israel'), the start of Jesus' ministry (as with the church's mission) *following on* from his experience in the Jerusalem Temple, the commencement of this sacred time being marked out by Satan's opportune departure (cf. 4:9–12, 13) and with Jesus' sermon in his home town of Nazareth (4:14–30 = the transposed Markan pericope Mk 6:1–6). Whatever you make of this explanation, the theory at least illustrates the very many interesting possibilities open to anyone who wishes to pursue redaction criticism on the Gospel of Luke!

Redaction criticism and the Gospel of Mark

Let us turn finally to the Gospel of Mark. There are difficulties involved in doing redaction criticism on Mark but these are not insuperable. Although no definite extensive written sources have been isolated for Mark, form criticism has enabled us to detect the traditional material used by Mark and to separate (to some extent) this traditional material from its Markan redaction. Most of the redaction criteria used in connection with Matthew and Luke can also, therefore, be applied to Mark.

Form-critical analysis reveals that the raw materials used by Mark were discrete, self-contained pericopae (or small clusters of pericopae) which represent the separate and diverse traditions about the nature and significance of Jesus' teaching, person and work. These have been selected, arranged and linked together – for the most part artificially – by the evangelist and then combined with a passion narrative to produce the first connected Gospel.

The main types and groupings of source material, and their location in the Gospel, are as follows:

1. Miracle stories: 1:21–45, 4:35–5:43, 6:35–52, 7:25–8:9, 22–26 (although cf. also the single pericopae of 9:14–27, 10:46–52 and 11:12–14, 20);
2. Controversy stories: 2:1–3:6, 3:20–35, 7:1–23, 11:27–12:40 (although cf. also the single pericopae of 8:11–13 and 10:2–9);
3. Parables: 4:1–33 (although cf. also the single pericopae of 12:1–11 and 13:34–36);
4. Teaching about discipleship: 8:27–10:45;
5. Apocalyptic discourse: 13;
6. Passion and resurrection narrative: 14–16.

The Markan material, moreover, is placed in a loose overall geographical framework, as follows:

1. Galilee: 1:14–5:43;
2. Galilee and the surrounding Gentile area (northern journey): 6:1–9:50;
3. Journey to Judaea and Jerusalem: 10:1–52;
4. Jerusalem: 11–16.

The redaction critic is interested, therefore, in the selection of the material, how it is arranged, how it is linked together, what special interests are shown by the evangelist and what redactional motifs run through the Gospel as a whole. Redaction critics are agreed on some eight features which characterize the Markan redaction.

The first is the evangelist's interest in Galilee. Jesus first appears there preaching the imminent coming of the kingdom of God (1:9, 14–15). He conducts his public ministry and mission in Galilee and receives an enthusiastic following there (1:28, 39, 3:7, 7:31, cf. also 9:30). He promises a post-resurrection appearance (or perhaps his *parousia*?) there (14:28, 16:7). All these 'Galilee' references (except 6:21) are redactional, according to W. Marxsen,[65] i.e. the evangelist *chose* to relate these traditions about Jesus to Galilee in the way he has done, and was not necessarily guided by the tradition to do so.

Two major theories have, therefore, been proposed to account for this interest. According to Marxsen himself, Mark's Gospel was composed in or near Galilee and written for a Palestinian Jewish-Christian community (*c.* 67–69 CE) which was awaiting Jesus' second coming in Galilee ('he is going before you to Galilee; there you will see him', Mk 16:7). An alternative theory is that of N. Perrin, who claimed that the use of Galilee is symbolic. Galilee had a large Gentile population, and was associated with the Gentiles (cf. Mt. 4:15 and Isa. 9:1, 'in the latter time he will make glorious the way of the sea, the land beyond Jordan,

Galilee of the nations'). 'Galilee' stands, therefore, for the Christian mission to the world, and in particular the Gentile mission.

Mark's interest in Gentiles and the Gentile mission is also reflected at other points in his Gospel. In chapter 7, verses 24–30, the evangelist has chosen to include a story relating one of Jesus' rare encounters with Gentiles, showing him being won over by the persistence and perspicacity of a Syro-Phoenician woman. In a redactional addendum to the parable of the vineyard (12:1–11), he makes Jesus refer obliquely to the new (Gentile) Israel which was to be the future Christian community ('What will the owner of the vineyard do? He will come and destroy the tenants, and give the vineyard to others', 12:9). Later, in the apocalyptic discourse, the prediction of a Gentile mission is made explicit ('And the gospel must first be preached to all nations', 13:10; cf. 13:27, 'he will . . . gather his elect . . . from the ends of the earth'). It is also adumbrated in the Markan Jesus' tribute to the anointing woman whose prescient action has anticipated his salvific death ('wherever the gospel is preached in the whole world, what she has done will be told in memory of her', 14:9). Not altogether surprisingly, then, when his death itself is recounted, the reader is informed that it is a Gentile centurion who declares Jesus to be the 'Son of God' (15:39) – the only human being within the Gospel itself to do so.

As some of the above references indicate, Mark is also fond of the word 'gospel' (the Greek word means 'good news') and, unlike the other evangelists, uses it frequently in his Gospel. Again all these references are redactional, according to Marxsen. His text opens with the words: 'The beginning of the *gospel* of Jesus Christ, the Son of God' (1:1); later in the same chapter, Jesus is cast (somewhat anachronistically, given its early church use as a technical term for the saving proclamation of Jesus' death and resurrection) in the role of a 'gospel preacher':

> Now after John was arrested, Jesus came into Galilee, preaching the gospel of God, and saying, 'The time is fulfilled, and the

kingdom of God is at hand; repent, and believe in the *gospel'*
(Mk 1:14–15; cf. also 8:35, 10:29).

A fourth feature of the evangelist's redaction is his symbolic use
of miracle stories. The miracles occur, for the most part, in the
first half of the Gospel. A number of them are found in two
(more or less) connected cycles in chapters 4 and 5 and in
chapters 6, 7 and 8. Mark appears to arrange those in chapters 7
and 8, however, so that they take place on Gentile soil. His
intention to group them in this way has been seen to reflect an
interest on his part once again in Gentiles and the Gentile mission.
The second feeding story (you will recall that there are two, one
in 6:30–44, the other in 8:1–10) may be for him the Gentile
counterpart of the first Jewish feeding miracle (cf. the enigmatic
passage 8:14–21 and the evangelist's invitation to the disciples –
and hence the reader – to discern the symbolic significance of
the numbers twelve and seven used in the stories). Mark is fond
of stories of the healing of those who are deaf, dumb or blind
(cf. e.g. 7:31–37, 8:22–26), stories that easily lend themselves to
spiritual application. One thinks of the 'blind man' story (8:22–26),
for example, which is placed immediately before the (unsuccess-
ful?) 'enlightenment' of the disciples (8:27–9:8). Another striking
use of symbolism comes with the cursing of the fig tree, the fate
of the unfruitful tree paralleling the fate of the Jerusalem Temple
(11:12–14, 15–19, 20–25, 13:1–2).

Significant also is Mark's use of controversy pericopae, stories
in which Jesus is found in conflict with certain opponents
(2:1–3:6, 3:20–35, 7:1–23, 8:11–13, 10:2–9, 11:27–12:40). He
presents Jesus engaged in disputes over a variety of issues with
a whole spectrum of contrasting Jewish leadership groups:
Pharisees, Herodians, Sadducees, chief priests, elders and scribes.
Many of these conflicts reflect controversies between the early
church and its opponents over issues such as fasting, sabbath
observance, the food laws, handwashing, etc. They have been

selected by the evangelist and incorporated into the Gospel, however, to provide an explanation to the Gospel's readers for the events leading up to the passion narrative and Jesus' crucifixion.

A sixth feature of the Gospel is its interest in the subject of true discipleship, persecution and martyrdom. This is reflected especially in chapters 8–10 (as well as in 13). In these chapters, the theme is Jesus' coming suffering and death. His future disciples, however, are also summoned to take up their crosses and follow him (cf. esp. 8:31–9:1). It is suggested, therefore, that Mark was written for a Gentile-Christian community experiencing persecution or even martyrdom for what was now termed (perhaps in light of the apostle Paul's influence) the 'gospel' (cf. esp. 8:35 and 13:9–13).

Mark was not only concerned with Jesus' future disciples – the Gentiles, who, as we have seen, came later to embrace the primitive but developing Christian faith – but also with Jesus' original Jewish disciples, the twelve. Commentators have long remarked on the harsh treatment they receive at the hands of the evangelist, a treatment softened by Matthew and Luke in their redaction. They bar others from coming to Jesus, or being reckoned among their group (9:38, 10:13–14). They are status-conscious (9:33–37, 10:28–31, 35–45). They are fearful, afraid, cowardly even (4:40–41, 6:50–51, 9:6, 32, 10:32, 14:50). They are exhorted to have faith, but admonished for the lack of it (4:40, 9:19, 11:22). For lack of faith, they are unable to perform miracles (9:18, 19, 23). Unable to keep watch in Gethsemane, one betrays him, others forsake him, another denies him (14:32–72). Unlike the true disciple (cf. 8:34–38), they are ashamed of him and fail to take up their cross and follow him. They are shown to be unaware of who Jesus really was, according to Mark, namely, the 'Son of God'. In the first part of the Gospel, they fail to comprehend this despite every invitation to do so. In the second part of the Gospel, they positively misunderstand the significance of Jesus' person and work.

This treatment of the disciples is part and parcel of a wider motif running through Mark's Gospel, namely, the secrecy motif, which constitutes our last, and, arguably, the most significant feature of the Gospel. This motif expresses itself essentially in three main ways.

First, there are the commands to silence. Jesus is shown, for example, *after exorcisms*, commanding demons to silence because they recognized that he was the Son of God (e.g. 3:11–12). He is shown *after healings* commanding the healed not to tell anyone about their cure (e.g. 1:43–44, 5:43, 7:36). He is shown *after the Caesarea confession scene* commanding the disciples not to spread it about that he was the Messiah (8:30).

Second, there is his secret instruction to the disciples. Jesus is represented as appearing repeatedly in private scenes with his disciples in which they are invited to understand the nature of his teaching and the significance of his person and work. Repeatedly, however, Mark shows us that they either fail to understand or positively misunderstand (e.g. 8:14–21, 32–33).

Third, there is Jesus' parabolic teaching. The reader is told by Mark that the purpose of Jesus' parables was not to *enlighten* his Jewish hearers, but to *mystify* them, not to reveal the truth to his audience, but to conceal it from them:

And he said to them, 'To you has been given the secret of the kingdom of God, but for those outside everything is in parables; so that they may indeed see but not perceive, and may indeed hear but not understand; lest they should turn again, and be forgiven' (4:10–12).

These observations were first brought to the attention of scholars by W. Wrede in *The Messianic Secret in the Gospels* (1901). How are they to be explained? Two main types of explanation are usually offered: historical explanations and literary/theological explanations. These explanations for the so-called 'Messianic Secret' are usually sought, moreover, at the three different levels of the tradition, and hence may be described as 'historical', 'traditional' and 'redactional' explanations.

Historical explanations account for the secrecy motif by an appeal to the primary level of the tradition, i.e. they claim that the secrecy attributed by the evangelist to Jesus and his behaviour actually goes back to Jesus himself. Jesus, they theorize, knew himself to be the Messiah but not in the popular Jewish sense, i.e. in a political sense. He wished to define his Messianic role differently, as one not involving or promoting war, violence and bloodshed. This was the view shared by a number of older scholars (e.g. V. Taylor, A. Schweitzer). But if the evangelist is accurately reporting Jesus' behaviour, various questions can be raised.

In the first place, why doesn't the Markan Jesus denounce the concept of a political Messiahship if that is what the secrecy injunctions are really all about? Why isn't Jesus' teaching on Messiahship more pronounced? In the second place, there are traditions in the Gospel in which Jesus appears to court or actively encourage popular Messianic conceptions (e.g. the triumphal entry and the cleansing of the temple). In the third place, if Jesus actually gave his disciples teaching on the true nature of his Messiahship, why did they misunderstand him? Viewed historically, their conduct is incomprehensible, even deplorable. Fourth, the prohibitions to secrecy are often quite senseless, if viewed historically (e.g. 5:43). Fifth, the motif appears, for the most part, though not exclusively, in redactional passages. Finally, we must ask why the motif is absent in the Gospel of John (where Jesus is shown openly proclaiming his intimate relationship with God) and played down by the other two evangelists Matthew and Luke.

Traditional explanations account for the secrecy motif by an appeal to the secondary level of the tradition, i.e. they claim that the secrecy attributed by the evangelists to Jesus goes back to the early church, and was introduced into the tradition about him in consequence of Christian theological hindsight. The early church first looked on Jesus as Messiah *after the resurrection*. The earliest traditions about him (i.e. those that go back to his lifetime) were non-Messianic therefore. To explain what was a later development in their thought about him, it was claimed by the early church, and subsequently by Mark, that he had actually kept his Messiahship a secret during his lifetime, divulging it only to his disciples. This was the view of W. Wrede. This position, too, has some drawbacks.

In the first place, if the earliest traditions were non-Messianic, then how again do we explain the presence in Mark of certain traditions which appear very early and yet which present Jesus as acting and speaking openly and not secretly as the Messiah (e.g. the triumphal entry and the cleansing of the temple in 11:1–11, 15–18 or Jesus' words before the High Priest at his trial, 14:61–62)? Second, how do we explain Jesus' crucifixion if it was not, in the primary tradition, that of a Messianic pretender? Third, how do we explain the fact that, although some very early traditions may have viewed Jesus as Messiah, Mark's readers are invited to share the secret that he was in fact the *Son of God* and not the Jewish *Messiah* (the two are not necessarily the same!). Fourth, in terms of Wrede's thesis, how do we explain the harsh treatment of the disciples in Mark?

Redactional explanations account for the secrecy motif by an appeal to the tertiary level of the tradition, i.e. they claim that the secrecy attributed by the evangelist to Jesus, while it may have already been present as a tendency in the tradition before Mark, was strongly developed by him, in order to promote his particular Christology. This view is supported by the fact that the secrecy motif appears, as we have noted, in redactional verses (though not exclusively so). Mark did not *introduce* a Christology (i.e. a particular understanding of who Jesus was) into his sources for these sources or traditions already reflected certain Christologies, and were already stamped with particular estimates of Jesus. The evangelist has merely used the secrecy motif to develop, counteract or qualify certain understandings of Jesus which already coloured the traditions he has taken over. This is the view of an increasing number of scholars, including myself (cf. e.g. J. B. Tyson, J. Schreiber, S. Schulz, T. J. Weeden, H. Räisänen). Mark himself was heir to both Hellenistic and Jewish traditions which already saw Jesus in a triumphalist light, namely as a wonder-working Hellenistic 'divine-man' (T. J. Weeden) or, more likely, a victorious Jewish Messianic figure, the Son of David (J. B. Tyson) or the returning, apocalyptic Son of Man. By means of the secrecy motif, and by building upon but qualifying these traditions, Mark invites his readers to see Jesus even more as the divine Son of God whose suffering and death on the cross were pre-ordained but whose divine status and mission as such had gone unrecognized (except by a Gentile, 15:39!) during his lifetime.

The 'Messianic Secret' in Mark, then, is a misnomer. We should instead talk of a 'Son of God' secret, for this is the true identity of Jesus, as the evangelist conceives it. By having Jesus act as the 'Son of God' incognito, and by imputing blindness and incomprehension regarding his identity to Jesus' original Jewish disciples, Mark, it would appear, has used the secrecy motif as a literary/theological device to qualify or even oppose an earlier Jewish–Christian Christology which regarded Jesus as the Davidic Messiah with a later more characteristically Gentile one that regarded him as the divine Son of God.

In conclusion, then, let us see what Mark has done. Throughout the Gospel he invites his readers to see Jesus as the Son of God. The Gospel begins with the words, 'The beginning of the Gospel of Jesus Christ, *the Son of God*' (1:1). The evangelist places this Christology (the secret) on the lips of God himself in two crucial scenes, the opening baptism of Jesus by John, and in the scene depicting Jesus' transfiguration before his disciples ('This is my beloved son', 1:11, 9:7). He intimates that Jesus' secret status as divine Son of God was recognized by the supernatural world, the demons (3:11, 5:7, etc.). It was also recognized, he tells the reader, by a Gentile, a Roman centurion, at the crucifixion, another climactic scene in the Gospel ('Truly this was the Son of God', 15:39). It was not recognized, on the other hand, by Jesus' original Jewish disciples. The most that Peter can come up with is his confession of Jesus as the Christ, the Jewish Messiah (8:29). Mark repeatedly points out to his readers, therefore, that the Christology of Jesus' original Jewish disciples, the twelve, was in error. They failed to understand, indeed, they misunderstood the true significance of Jesus' person and work. At no point, even at the end of the Gospel, are they shown finally to come to this understanding. The conclusion that some scholars have suspected, and that I myself have increasingly come to draw, is that the author of the Gospel of Mark writes as a representative of a Pauline-influenced Gentile Christianity which viewed Jesus as a divine being over against the claims of an original Jewish Christianity which, in keeping with its monotheism, saw Jesus as the Jewish Messiah – either as a human and in large part a mainly political figure, or as a transcendent figure who as Son of Man was about to return to this earth – but not as the *Son of God*, a divine figure, an epiphany of God, the one indeed whom later Christianity was to see as the very incarnation of God himself.

★★★

Our redaction–critical examination of the Synoptic Gospels is complete, and so is this *The New Testament: A Beginner's Guide*. In my opening chapter, I likened the process of understanding the New Testament to archaeology. I hope that now you will have a much greater knowledge of these fascinating texts, and a more sophisticated appreciation of the many layers of history and theology which they reflect. We have taken an aerial view of the world of the New Testament, and by a series of ever-narrowing circles, have focused in turn on the origins and history of the early church, and the nature and development of early Christian belief and practice. We have looked at the factors which led to the emergence of the New Testament writings, and I have given you a brief introduction to them. Finally, as promised, we have done some digging in one corner of the field. Using the tools of source, form and redaction criticism, we have excavated the Synoptic Gospels, and have attempted to uncover the sources, both written and oral, which underlie them, as well as expose the historical setting, literary skill and religious motivations of the evangelists who composed them. The New Testament writings are a fascinating field of enquiry and a never-ending source of interest. I trust that this *Beginner's Guide* has provided you with the knowledge and skills to pursue further explorations, and I wish you, the reader, many exciting discoveries!

Notes

1. N. Perrin, *The New Testament. An Introduction. Proclamation and Parenesis, Myth and History* (New York: Harcourt Brace Jovanovich, 1982), p. 502.
2. A. Roberts and W. B. Rambaut (eds), *The Writings of Irenaeus*, Ante-Nicene Christian Library. Translations of the Writings of the Fathers Down to A.D. 325 (Edinburgh: T. & T. Clark, 1868), vol. I, p. 478.
3. See L. Alexander (ed.), *Images of Empire*, Journal for the Study of the Old Testament Supplement Series, 122 (Sheffield: JSOT, 1991).
4. Tacitus, *Agricola*, Loeb Classical Library (New York, NY and London: Macmillan; Heinemann, 1914), p. 221.
5. See, for example, F. G. Downing, *Cynics and Christian Origins* (Edinburgh: T. & T. Clark, 1992).
6. Apuleius, *Metamorphoses*, Loeb Classical Library (London and New York: Heinemann; Macmillan, 1914), pp. 545–547. *Gratia* W. Barclay, 'A Comparison of Paul's Missionary Preaching and his Preaching to the Church' in W. W. Gasque and R. P. Martin (eds), *Apostolic History and the Gospel. New Testament Essays Presented to E. F. Bruce* (Exeter: Paternoster, 1970), p. 171.
7. A striking reconstruction of a *mithraeum*, taken from Carrawburgh, near Hadrian's Wall, can be seen at the Museum of Antiquities at the University of Newcastle.
8. For a famous example, see Philostratus, *Life of Apollonius of Tyana*, IV.20, Loeb Classical Library (London and New York: Heinemann; Macmillan, 1912), vol. I, pp. 388–393.

9. For an example in connection with the Emperor Vespasian, see D. R. Cartlidge and D. L. Dungan, *Documents for the Study of the Gospels* (Cleveland, OH, New York and London: Collins, 1980), p. 156.

10. See, for example, A. Harnack, *History of Dogma* (London: Williams & Norgate, 1897), vol. 1, pp. 222–265, and especially p. 226: '. . . the Gnostic systems represent the acute secularising or hellenising of Christianity, with the rejection of the Old Testament'.

11. The Jewish background to Christianity is now stressed much more than it used to be in New Testament scholarship. Compare, for example, the influential works of E. P. Sanders, *Paul and Palestinian Judaism* (Philadelphia, PA: Fortress, 1977) and *Jesus and Judaism* (Philadelphia, PA and London: Fortress; SCM, 1985). In using the expression 'Jewish background', however, as Jewish scholars such as G. Vermes have reminded us, we must avoid any impression that currents in first-century Judaism, or the Jewish sources of this period, are only of interest or importance insofar as they shed light on the origins of Christianity. Attention to the 'Jewish background', however, forcibly reminds us that in studying the origins of Christianity, before the so-called 'parting of the ways', we are in effect, studying first-century Judaism, in one of its many fascinating manifestations.

12. The same writer (i.e. Justin Martyr) mentions the war of that time against the Jews and makes this observation, 'For in the present Jewish war it was only Christians whom Bar Chocheba, the leader of the rebellion of the Jews, commanded to be punished severely, if they did not deny Jesus as the Messiah and blaspheme him.' Cited Eusebius, *Ecclesiastical History*, IV.viii.4, Loeb Classical Library (Cambridge, MA and London: Harvard University Press; Heinemann, 1965) vol. I, p. 323.

13. See Josephus, *The Jewish War*, Loeb Classical Library (London and New York: Heinemann; Putnam, 1927/1928), vol. II, pp. 389–391.

14. The Temple inscription mentioned here by Josephus warning Gentiles on pain of death from proceeding beyond the court reserved for them was discovered in 1871. See C. K. Barrett, *The New Testament Background. Selected Documents* (London: SPCK, 1957), p. 50.

15. See E. Lohse, *The New Testament Environment*, New Testament Library (London: SCM, 1975), p. 150. The view of Lohse, with regard to women's participation in synagogue worship, is beginning to be challenged, it should be noted. See, for example, the article by S. Safrai, 'The Place of Women in First Century Synagogues', *Jerusalem Perspective*, 40, 1993. A full and cautious assessment of the evidence is given by W. Horbury who states, to the contrary, that '[w]omen took part in synagogue services in the ancient world, and sometimes received official titles like "ruler of the synagogue" or "elder"'. He adds the caveat, however, that 'interpretation is hampered by lack of detailed information on the ancient synagogue'. See W. Horbury, 'Women in the Synagogue' in W. Horbury, W. D. Davies and J. Sturdy (eds), *The Cambridge History of Judaism* (Cambridge: Cambridge University Press, 1999), pp. 358–401, esp. p. 358.

16. Josephus, *Jewish Antiquities*, Loeb Classical Library (London and Cambridge, MA: Heinemann; Harvard University Press, 1963/1965), pp. 9, 20–21; *The Jewish War*, Loeb Classical Library (London and New York: Heinemann; Putnam, 1927/1928), p. 369.

17. Translations of, or selections from a number of these sources can be consulted, for example, in the following: J. Stevenson, *A New Eusebius: Documents Illustrative of the History of the Church to A.D. 337* (London: SPCK, 1968); H. Bettenson (ed.), *Documents of the Christian Church* (Oxford: Oxford

University Press, 1963); C. K. Barrett, *The New Testament Background. Selected Documents* (London: SPCK, 1987); H. C. Kee, *The Origins of Christianity. Sources and Documents* (London: SPCK, 1980); D. R. Cartlidge and D. L. Dungan, *Documents for the Study of the Gospels* (Cleveland, OH, New York and London: Collins, 1980); E. Hennecke and W. Schneemelcher (eds), *New Testament Apocrypha* (London: SCM, 1963).

18. Cited in Stevenson, *New Eusebius*, pp. 2–3.

19. Cited ibid., p. 3.

20. Pliny, *Letters*, Loeb Classical Library (New York, NY and London: Macmillan; Heinemann, 1915), X.96 & 97. Cited in Stevenson, *New Eusebius*, pp. 13–16. See below, p. 41.

21. A translation of these passages can be found in Josephus, *The Jewish War* (Harmondsworth, UK: Penguin, 1970), trans. G. A. Williamson, pp. 396–401.

22. See D. C. Duling and N. Perrin, *The New Testament. Proclamation and Parenesis, Myth and History* (New York: Harcourt Brace College, 1994), pp. 420, 512–516.

23. See Eusebius, *Ecclesiastical History*, Loeb Classical Library (2 volumes; London and New York: Heinemann; Putnam, 1926, 1932).

24. C. H. Dodd, *The Apostolic Preaching and its Developments* (London: Hodder & Stoughton, 1936), pp. 38–45.

25. Duling and Perrin, *The New Testament* (1994), p. 114.

26. See N. Perrin, *The New Testament. An Introduction. Proclamation and Parenesis, Myth and History* (New York: Harcourt Brace Jovanovich, 1982), pp. 71–72.

27. See S. G. F. Brandon, *The Fall of Jerusalem and the Christian Church* (London: SPCK, 1951); cf. also his *Jesus and the Zealots. A Study of the Political Factor in Primitive Christianity* (Manchester: Manchester University Press, 1967), pp. 146–220.

28. See the accounts by Clement of Rome, Eusebius and Sulpicius Severus in Stevenson, *New Eusebius*, pp. 4–6.

29. See Brandon, *Zealots*, p. 209, n. 1 and references cited there.

30. Cited in Stevenson, *New Eusebius*, pp. 13–14.

31. P. M. Casey, *From Jewish Prophet to Gentile God. The Origins and Development of New Testament Christology* (Cambridge, UK and Louisville, KY: Clarke; Westminster/John Knox, 1991). This interpretation of developments in New Testament Christology, of course, is not shared by all scholars. For contrasting views, see, for example, R. Bauckham, *God Crucified. Monotheism and Christology in the New Testament* (Didsbury Lectures; Carlisle: Paternoster, 1998) and L. W. Hurtado, *One God, One Lord. Early Christian Devotion and Ancient Jewish Monotheism* (Philadelphia, PA: Fortress, 1988).

32. See C. H. Dodd, *According to the Scriptures. The Sub-Structure of New Testament Theology* (London: Nisbet, 1952).

33. J. A. T. Robinson, *Redating the New Testament* (London: SCM, 1976).

34. Although the boundary is fluid, the 'letter' emerges from a concrete situation, with specific interests or concerns in mind. The 'epistle', on the other hand, is a theological treatise availing itself of the letter form, a deliberate literary creation intended for wide dissemination and not concerned primarily with a concrete situation or audience.

35. A fresh reassessment of the nature and importance of this notion for the understanding of Paul's thought with relation to Judaism is to be found in the widely influential and hitherto mentioned book by E. P. Sanders, *Paul and Palestinian Judaism* (Philadelphia, PA: Fortress, 1977).

36. See R. H. Fuller, *A Critical Introduction to the New Testament* (London: Duckworth, 1966), p. 195.

37. See also the description given by Eusebius (*Eccl. Hist.* III.17–20, cited Stevenson, *New Eusebius*, p. 9) of the descendants of the family of Jesus in the reign of Domitian.

38. Eusebius, *Eccl. Hist.* III.39.4. Cited Stevenson, *New Eusebius*, p. 50.

39. See, for example, B. D. Ehrman, *The New Testament. A Historical Introduction to the Early Christian Writings* (New York: Oxford University Press, 1999); R. E. Brown, *An Introduction to the New Testament*, Anchor Bible Reference Library (New York: Doubleday, 1997); D. C. Duling and N. Perrin, *The New Testament. Proclamation and Parenesis, Myth and History* (New York: Harcourt Brace College, 1994); W. D. Davies, *Invitation to the New Testament. A Guide to Its Main Witnesses*, The Biblical Seminar, 19 (Sheffield: Sheffield Academic Press, 1993); R. F. Collins, *Introduction to the New Testament*, The Anchor Bible (Garden City, NY and London: Doubleday; SCM, 1983); W. G. Kümmel, *Introduction to the New Testament* (London: SCM, 1979); G. Bornkamm, *The New Testament. A Guide to its Writings* (Philadelphia, PA: Fortress, 1973); W. Marxsen, *Introduction to the New Testament. An Approach to its Problems* (Oxford: Blackwell, 1968); R. H. Fuller, *A Critical Introduction to the New Testament* (London: Duckworth, 1966); H. C. Kee, F. W. Young and K. Froehlich, *Understanding the New Testament* (London: Darton, Longman & Todd, 1963). A particularly succinct and helpful treatment is to be found in C. F. Evans, 'The New Testament in the Making' in P. R. Ackroyd and C. F. Evans (eds), *The Cambridge History of the Bible. Vol. I: From the Beginnings to Jerome* (Cambridge, UK: Cambridge University Press, 1970), pp. 232–284.

40. Compare, however, the case made by R. Bauckham that both Jude (*Jude and the Relatives of Jesus in the Early Church* (Edinburgh: T. & T. Clark, 1990)), and James (*James: Wisdom of James, Disciple of Jesus the Sage* (New Testament Readings; London and New York: Routledge, 1999)) were indeed written by the brothers of Jesus.

41. Fuller, *Critical Introduction*, p. 144.

42. For a succinct account of the origin and history of the New Testament canon, see F. W. Beare, 'Canon of the NT' in

G. A. Buttrick (ed.), *The Interpreter's Dictionary of the Bible* (New York and Nashville: Abingdon, 1962), pp. 520–532.

43. For a translation of these, see M. Staniforth (ed.), *Early Christian Writings. The Apostolic Fathers*, Penguin Classics (Harmondsworth, MX: Penguin, 1968).

44. Nashville, TN and New York: Nelson, 1979.

45. Classic form critics tended to speak of the 'laws' of oral transmission, a view now discredited given the lack of consistent directionality in the developing tradition, and the evidence of contrary examples to perceived trends. See E. P. Sanders, *The Tendencies of the Synoptic Tradition*, Society for New Testament Studies Monograph Series, 9 (Cambridge, UK: Cambridge University Press, 1969). Despite Sanders' forcible attack on the classical form-critical position in this regard, there is some merit, in my opinion, in retaining the term 'tendency', if not the word 'law', since it does imply some fluidity in the tradition, and yet encourages us to seek and identify the phenomenon of imaginative embellishment, as here, in its varying forms.

46. See Davies, *Invitation*, p. 103.

47. K. L. Schmidt, *Der Rahmen des Geschichte Jesu. Literarkritische Untersuchungen zur ältesten Jesusüberlieferung* (Berlin: Trowitzsch & Sohn, 1919).

48. A good summary of Bultmann's otherwise difficult *The History of the Synoptic Tradition* is to be found in an essay he wrote to which I am indebted. This was translated by F. C. Grant and appeared in R. Bultmann and K. Kundsin, *Form Criticism. Two Essays on New Testament Research* (New York: Harper, 1962).

49. S. H. Travis, 'Form Criticism' in I. H. Marshall (ed.), *New Testament Interpretation* (Exeter: Paternoster, 1977), p. 157.

50. For a review of its limitations, see Travis in *New Testament Interpretation*, pp. 157–160.

51. See Dodd, *Apostolic Preaching*.

52. See Fuller, *Critical Introduction*, p. 93.

53. See W. R. Farmer. *The Synoptic Problem: A Critical Analysis* (Dillsboro, NC: Western North Carolina Press, 1976), esp. pp. 5–9 where Griesbach's hypothesis is discussed. For a rebuttal of this solution, see C. M. Tuckett, *The Revival of the Griesbach Hypothesis. An Analysis and Appraisal,* Society for New Testament Studies Monograph Series, 44 (Cambridge, UK: Cambridge University Press, 1983).

54. See B. C. Butler, *The Originality of St Matthew. A Critique of the Two-Document Hypothesis* (Cambridge: Cambridge University Press, 1951); J. Chapman, *Matthew, Mark and Luke* (London: Longmans, Green and Co., 1937).

55. G. M. Styler, 'The Priority of Mark' in C. F. D. Moule (ed.), *The Birth of the New Testament* (London: Black, 1966), p. 231 (Excursus IV).

56. See, for example, D. R. Catchpole, *The Quest for Q* (Edinburgh: T. & T. Clark, 1993); C. M. Tuckett, *Q and the History of Early Christianity. Studies on Q.* (Edinburgh: T. & T. Clark, 1996).

57. See, for example, M. D. Goulder, *Midrash and Lection in Matthew* (London: SPCK, 1974) and A. Farrer, 'On Dispensing with Q' in D. E. Nineham (ed.), *Studies in the Gospels. Essays in Memory of R. H. Lightfoot* (Oxford: Blackwell, 1955), pp. 55–86.

58. B. H. Streeter, *The Four Gospels. A Study of Origins* (London: Macmillan, 1924).

59. M. Dibelius, *From Tradition to Gospel* (London: Ivor Nicholson & Watson, 1934), p. 3.

60. R. H. Stein, 'What is *Redaktionsgeschichte?*', *Journal of Biblical Literature*, 88 (1969), p. 46.

61. R. T. Fortna, 'Redaction Criticism, NT' in K. Crim (ed.), *Interpreter's Dictionary of the Bible, Supplementary Volume* (Nashville: Abingdon, 1976), p. 733.

62. G. Bornkamm, G. Barth and H. J. Held, *Tradition and Interpretation in Matthew* (London: SCM, 1963); H. Conzelmann, *The Theology of St Luke* (London: Faber, 1960);

W. Marxsen, *Mark the Evangelist. Studies on the Redaction History of the Gospel* (Nashville, New York and London: Abingdon; SPCK, 1969).

63. W. Wrede, *The Messianic Secret* (The Library of Theological Translations; Cambridge and London: Clarke, 1971); E. Lohmeyer, *Das Evangelium des Markus* (Kritisch-exegetischer Kommentar über das Neue Testament; Göttingen: Vandenhoeck & Ruprecht, 1963); R. H. Lightfoot, *History and Interpretation in the Gospels* (London: Hodder & Stoughton, 1934).

64. See G. Bornkamm, G. Barth and H. J. Held, *Tradition and Interpretation in Matthew* (London: SCM, 1963).

65. See W. Marxsen, *Mark the Evangelist. Studies on the Redaction History of the Gospel* (Nashville, New York and London: Abingdon; SPCK, 1969), pp. 54–116.

Further reading

Chapter 1: The world of the New Testament

The Roman Empire

Balsdon, J. P. V. D. 'The Roman Empire in the First Century' in M. Black and H. H. Rowley (eds), *Peake's Commentary on the Bible*, London, Nelson, 1962, pp. 699–704

Barrett, C. K. *The New Testament Background. Selected Documents.* London, SPCK, 1957

Bruce, F. F. *New Testament History*. London, Nelson, 1969

Cartlidge, D. R. and D. L. Dungan. *Documents for the Study of the Gospels*. Cleveland, OH, New York and London, Collins, 1980

Filson, F. V. *A New Testament History*. London, SCM, 1965

Grant, R. M. 'Roman Empire' in G. A. Buttrick (ed.), *The Interpreter's Dictionary of the Bible*, New York and Nashville, TN, Abingdon, 1962, pp. 103–109

Kraybill, J. N. *Imperial Cult and Commerce in John's Apocalypse*, Journal for the Study of the New Testament Supplement Series, 132, Sheffield, Sheffield Academic Press, 1996

Sherwin-White, A. N. *Roman Society and the Roman Law in the New Testament*, The Sarum Lectures, 1960–61. New York and London, Oxford University Press, 1963

Barclay, W. 'Hellenistic Thought in New Testament Times', *Expository Times*, 71 and 72 (1959–60), 71, 207–209 ('The New Emphasis, Part 1'), 246–248 ('The New Emphasis, Part 2'), 280–284 ('The New Emphasis, Part 3'), 297–301 ('The Sceptics'), 371–375 ('The Cynics'), 29–31 ('Cyreniacs'),

78–31 ('Epicureans, Part 1'), 101–104 ('Epicureans, Part 2'), 146–149 ('Epicureans, Part 3'), 164–166 ('Stoics, Part 1'), 200–203 ('Stoics, Part 2'), 227–230 ('Stoics, Part 3'), 258–261 ('Stoics, Part 4'), 291–294 ('Stoics, Part 5')

Barrett, C. K. *The New Testament Background. Selected Documents.* London, SPCK, 1957

Bruce, F. F. *New Testament History.* London, Nelson, 1969

Bultmann, R. *Primitive Christianity in its Contemporary Context.* London, Thames and Hudson, 1956

Cartlidge, D. R. and D. L. Dungan. *Documents for the Study of the Gospels.* Cleveland, OH, New York and London, Collins, 1980

Cook, M. J. 'Judaism, Hellenistic' in K. Crim (ed.), *The Interpreter's Dictionary of the Bible, Supplementary Volume*, Nashville, TN, Abingdon, 1976, pp. 505–509

Filson, F. V. A *New Testament History.* London, SCM, 1965

Grant, F. C. 'Hellenism' in G. A. Buttrick (ed.), *The Interpreter's Dictionary of the Bible*, New York and Nashville, TN, Abingdon, 1962, p. 580

Kee, H. C., F. W. Young and K. Froehlich. *Understanding the New Testament.* London, Darton, Longman & Todd, 1963

Kee, H. C. *The Origins of Christianity. Sources and Documents.* London, SPCK, 1980

Kee, H. C. *Christian Origins in Sociological Perspective.* London, SCM, 1980

Peters, F. E. 'Hellenism' in K. Crim (ed.), *The Interpreter's Dictionary of the Bible, Supplementary Volume*, Nashville, TN, Abingdon, 1976, pp. 395–401

Stambaugh, J. and D. Balch. *The Social World of the First Christians.* London, SPCK, 1986

Wilson, R. M. 'Pagan Religion at the Coming of Christianity' in M. Black and H. H. Rowley (eds), *Peake's Commentary on the Bible,* London, Nelson, 1962, pp. 712–718

Wilson, R. M. 'Slippery Words: Gnosis, Gnostic, Gnosticism', *Expository Times,* 89(1978–79), pp. 296–301

Barrett, C. K. *The New Testament Background. Selected Documents.* London, SPCK, 1957

Betz, O. 'Essenes' in K. Crim (ed.), *The Interpreter's Dictionary of the Bible, Supplementary Volume,* Nashville, Abingdon, 1976, pp. 277–279

Black, M. 'Pharisees' in G. A. Buttrick (ed.), *The Interpreter's Dictionary of the Bible,* New York/Nashville, Abingdon, 1962, pp. 774–781

Black, M. 'The Development of Judaism in the Greek and Roman Periods' in M. Black and H. H. Rowley (eds), *Peake's Commentary on the Bible,* London, Nelson, 1962, pp. 693–698

Brandon, S. G. F. *Jesus and the Zealots. A Study of the Political Factor in Primitive Christianity.* Manchester, Manchester University Press, 1967

Bruce, F. F. *New Testament History.* London, Nelson, 1969

Buchanan, G. W. 'Essenes' in G. W. Bromiley (ed.), *The International Standard Bible Encyclopedia,* Grand Rapids, MI, Eerdmans, 1986, pp. 147–155

Cartlidge, D. R. and D. L. Dungan. *Documents for the Study of the Gospels.* Cleveland, OH, New York and London, Collins, 1980

Chilton, B. and J. Neusner. *Judaism in the New Testament. Practices and Beliefs.* London and New York, Routledge, 1995

Cook, M. J. 'Judaism, Early Rabbinic' in K. Crim (ed.), *The Interpreter's Dictionary of the Bible, Supplementary Volume,* Nashville, TN, Abingdon, 1976, pp. 499–505

Cook, M. J. 'Judaism, Hellenistic' in K. Crim (ed.), *The Interpreter's Dictionary of the Bible, Supplementary Volume,* Nashville, TN, Abingdon, 1976, pp. 505–509

Davies, W. D. 'Contemporary Jewish Religion' in M. Black and H. H. Rowley (eds), *Peake's Commentary on the Bible,* London, Nelson, 1962, pp. 705–711

Donaldson, T. L. 'Zealot' in G. W. Bromiley (ed.), *The International Standard Bible Encyclopedia,* Grand Rapids, MI, Eerdmans, 1986, pp. 1175–1179

Farmer, W. R. 'Essenes' in G. A. Buttrick (ed.), *The Interpreter's Dictionary of the Bible*, New York/Nashville: Abingdon, 1962, pp. 143–149

Farmer, W. R. 'Zealot' in G. A. Buttrick (ed.), *The Interpreter's Dictionary of the Bible*, New York/Nashville, Abingdon, 1962, pp. 936–939

Filson, F. V. *A New Testament History*. London, SCM, 1965

Heard, W. J. 'Revolutionary Movements' in J. B. Green, S. McKnight and I. H. Marshall (eds), *Dictionary of Jesus and the Gospels*, Downers Grove, IL, InterVarsity Press, 1992, pp. 688–698

Hengel, M. *Judaism and Hellenism. Studies in their Encounter in Palestine during the Early Hellenistic Period*. London, SCM, 1974

Kee, H. C., F. W. Young and K. Froehlich. *Understanding the New Testament*. London, Darton, Longman & Todd, 1963

Kee, H. C. *The Origins of Christianity. Sources and Documents*. London, SPCK, 1980

Kee, H. C. *Christian Origins in Sociological Perspective*. London, SCM, 1980

Lieu, J. 'Pharisees and Scribes' in R. J. Coggins and J. L. Houlden (eds), *A Dictionary of Biblical Interpretation*, London and Philadelphia, PA, SCM/Trinity Press International, 1990, pp. 537–539

Martinez, F. G. and J. T. Barrera. *The People of the Dead Sea Scrolls. Their Writings, Beliefs and Practices*. Leiden, New York and Cologne, Brill, 1993

Merkel, H. 'Zealot' in K. Crim (ed.), *The Interpreter's Dictionary of the Bible, Supplementary Volume*, Nashville, Abingdon, 1976, pp. 979–982

Moulder, W. J. 'Sadducees' in G. W. Bromiley (ed.), *The International Standard Bible Encyclopedia*, Grand Rapids, MI, Eerdmans, 1986, pp. 271–278

Neusner, J. *Judaism in the Beginning of Christianity*. London, SPCK, 1984

Pope, M. H. "Am Ha'aretz' in G. A. Buttrick (ed.), *The Interpreter's Dictionary of the Bible*, New York/Nashville, Abingdon, 1962, pp. 106–107

Reicke, B. *The New Testament Era. The World of the Bible from 500 B.C. to A.D. 100*. London, Black, 1978

Rivkin, E. 'Pharisees' in K. Crim (ed.), *The Interpreter's Dictionary of the Bible, Supplementary Volume*, Nashville, Abingdon, 1976, pp. 657–663

Rowland, C. C. *Christian Origins. An Account of the Setting and Character of the most Important Messianic Sect of Judaism*. London, SPCK, 1985

Russell, D. S. *The Jews from Alexander to Herod*, New Clarendon Bible, Old Testament, 5. Oxford, Oxford University Press, 1967

Stambaugh, J. and D. Balch. *The Social World of the First Christians*. London, SPCK, 1986

Sanders, E. P. *Paul and Palestinian Judaism*. Philadelphia, PA, Fortress, 1977

Sanders, E. P. *Jesus and Judaism*. Philadelphia, PA and London, Fortress/SCM, 1985

Sundberg, A. C. 'Sadducees' in G. A. Buttrick (ed.), *The Interpreter's Dictionary of the Bible*, New York/Nashville, Abingdon, 1962, pp. 160–163

Vermes, G. 'Dead Sea Scrolls' in K. Crim (ed.), *The Interpreter's Dictionary of the Bible, Supplementary Volume*. Nashville, Abingdon, 1976, pp. 210–219

Westerholm, S. 'Pharisees' in J. B. Green, S. McKnight and I. H. Marshall (eds), *Dictionary of Jesus and the Gospels*. Downers Grove, IL, InterVarsity Press, 1992, pp. 609–614

Wyatt, R. J. 'Pharisees' in G. W. Bromiley (ed.), *The International Standard Bible Encyclopedia*, Grand Rapids, MI, Eerdmans, 1986, pp. 822–829

Chapter 2: The early church

The origins and history of the early church

Bettenson, H. (ed.). *Documents of the Christian Church*. Oxford, Oxford University Press, 1963

Brandon, S. G. F. *The Fall of Jerusalem and the Christian Church*. London, SPCK, 1951

Brown, S. *The Origins of Christianity. A Historical Introduction to the New Testament*. Oxford, Oxford University Press, 1984

Bruce, F. F. *New Testament History*. London, Nelson, 1969

Caird, G. B. *The Apostolic Age*. London, Duckworth, 1955

Elliott, J. K. *Questioning Christian Origins*. London, SCM, 1982

Filson, F. V. *A New Testament History*. London, SCM, 1965

Frend, W. H. C. *The Early Church*. London, Hodder, 1965

Reicke, B. *The New Testament Era. The World of the Bible from 500 B.C. to A.D. 100*. London, Black, 1978

Rowland, C. C. *Christian Origins. An Account of the Setting and Character of the Most Important Messianic Sect of Judaism*. London, SPCK, 1985

Stevenson, J. A. *New Eusebius: Documents illustrative of the History of the Church to A.D. 337*. London, SPCK, 1968

Theissen, G. *The First Followers of Jesus / Sociology of Early Palestinian Christianity*. London and Philadelphia, SCM/Fortress, 1978

Tidball, D. *An Introduction to the Sociology of the New Testament*. Exeter, Paternoster, 1983

The nature and development of early christian belief and practice

Barclay, W. *The Lord's Supper*. London, SCM, 1967

Beasley-Murray, G. R. *Baptism in the New Testament*. London and New York, Macmillan/St. Martin's, 1962

Cullmann, O. *Baptism in the New Testament*, Studies in Biblical Theology. London, SCM, 1950

Cullmann, O. *Early Christian Worship*, Studies in Biblical Theology. London, SCM, 1953

Dodd, C. H. *The Apostolic Preaching and its Developments*. London, Hodder & Stoughton, 1936

Dunn, J. D. G. *Unity and Diversity in the New Testament. An Inquiry into the Character of Earliest Christianity*. London, SCM, 1977

Fiorenza, E. S. 'Eschatology of the NT' in K. Crim (ed.), *The Interpreter's Dictionary of the Bible, Supplementary Volume*, Nashville, TN, Abingdon, 1976, pp. 271–277

Houlden, J. L. *Ethics and the New Testament*, London and Oxford, Penguin/Mowbray, 1973

Jeremias, J. *The Eucharistic Words of Jesus*. Oxford, Blackwell, 1955

Käsemann, E. 'Ministry and Community in the New Testament' in *Essays on New Testament Themes*. London, SCM, 1964, pp. 63–94

McArthur, H. K. 'Parousia' in G. A. Buttrick (ed.), *The Interpreter's Dictionary of the Bible*, New York and Nashville, TN, Abingdon, 1962, pp. 658–661

Menoud, P. H. 'Church, Life and Organization of' in G. A. Buttrick (ed.), *The Interpreter's Dictionary of the Bible*, New York and Nashville, TN, Abingdon, 1962, pp. 617–626

Schweizer, E. *Church Order in the New Testament*, Studies in Biblical Theology. London, SCM, 1963

Chapter 3: The New Testament

The emergence of the New Testament

Barclay, W. *The Making of the Bible*, Bible Guides, 1. London, New York and Nashville, TN, Lutterworth/Abingdon, 1961

Beare, F. W. 'Canon of the N.T.' in G. A. Buttrick (ed.), *The Interpreter's Dictionary of the Bible*, New York and Nashville, Abingdon, 1962, pp. 520–532

Evans, C. F. 'The New Testament in the Making' in P. R. Ackroyd and C. F. Evans (eds), *The Cambridge History of the Bible. Vol. I: From the Beginnings to Jerome*, Cambridge, UK, Cambridge University Press, 1970, pp. 232–284

Grant, F. C. *The Gospels: Their Origin and their Growth*. London, Faber & Faber, 1957

Moule, C. F. D. *The Birth of the New Testament*, Black's New Testament Commentaries, Companion Volume, 1. London, Black, 1966

Staniforth, M. (ed.). *Early Christian Writings. The Apostolic Fathers*, Penguin Classics. Harmondsworth, MX, Penguin, 1968

A brief introduction to the New Testament writings

Bornkamm, G. *The New Testament. A Guide to its Writings*. Philadelphia, PA, Fortress, 1973

Brown, R. E. *An Introduction to the New Testament,* Anchor Bible Reference Library. New York, Doubleday, 1997

Collins, R. F. *Introduction to the New Testament,* The Anchor Bible. Garden City, NY and London, Doubleday/SCM, 1983

Duling, D. C. and N. Perrin. *The New Testament. Proclamation and Parenesis. Myth and History*. New York, Harcourt Brace College, 1994

Ehrman, B. D. *The New Testament. A Historical Introduction to the Early Christian Writings*. New York, Oxford University Press, 1999

Fuller, R. H. *A Critical Introduction to the New Testament*. London, Duckworth, 1966

Kümmel, W. G. *Introduction to the New Testament*. London, SCM, 1979

Marxsen, W. *Introduction to the New Testament. An Approach to its Problems*. Oxford, Blackwell, 1968

Robinson, J. A. T. *Redating the New Testament*. London, SCM, 1976

Wikenhauser, A. *New Testament Introduction*. New York and Edinburgh, Herder & Herder/Nelson, 1958

Chapter 4: Interpreting the Gospels: Hermeneutics

Form criticism

Barbour, R. S. *Traditio-Historical Criticism of the Gospels*. London, SCM, 1972

Bultmann, R. and K. Kundsin. *Form Criticism. Two Essays on New Testament Research*. New York, Harper, 1962

Bultmann, R. *The History of the Synoptic Tradition*. Oxford, Blackwell, 1968

Carlston, C. E. 'Form Criticism, NT' in K. Crim (ed.), *The Interpreter's Dictionary of the Bible, Supplementary Volume*, Nashville, TN, Abingdon, 1976, pp. 345–348

Dibelius, M. *From Tradition to Gospel*. London, Ivor Nicholson & Watson, 1934

Dinkler, E. 'Form Criticism of the New Testament' in M. Black and H. H. Rowley (eds), *Peake's Commentary on the Bible*, London, Nelson, 1962, pp. 683–685

Grobel, K. 'Biblical Criticism' in G. A. Buttrick (ed.), *The Interpreter's Dictionary of the Bible*, New York and Nashville, Abingdon, 1962, pp. 407–413

Hayes, J. H. and C. R. Holladay. *Biblical Exegesis. A Beginner's Handbook*. London, SCM, 1982

Henry, P. *New Directions in New Testament Study*. London, SCM, 1980

Marshall, I. H. (ed.). *New Testament Interpretation*. Exeter, Paternoster, 1977

McKnight, E. V., *What is Form Criticism?*, Guides to Biblical Scholarship, New Testament Series. Philadelphia, PA, Fortress, 1969

Sanders, E. P. *The Tendencies of the Synoptic Tradition*, Society for New Testament Studies Monograph Series, 9. Cambridge, UK, Cambridge University Press, 1969

Sanders, E. P. and M. Davies. *Studying the Synoptic Gospels*. London and Philadelphia, PA, SCM/Trinity Press International, 1989

Taylor, V. *The Formation of the Gospel Tradition*. London, Macmillan, 1933

Travis, S. H. 'Form Criticism' in I. H. Marshall (ed.), *New Testament Interpretation*, Exeter, Paternoster, 1977, pp. 153–164

Tuckett, C. M. *Reading the New Testament*. London, SPCK, 1987

Source criticism, the Synoptic problem and the emergence of redaction criticism

Butler, B. C. *The Originality of St Matthew. A Critique of the Two-Document Hypothesis*. Cambridge, Cambridge University Press, 1951

Catchpole, D. R. *The Quest for Q*. Edinburgh, T. & T. Clark, 1993

Chapman, J. *Matthew, Mark and Luke*. London, Longmans, Green and Co., 1937

Farmer, W. R. *The Synoptic Problem: a Critical Analysis*. Dillsboro, NC: Western North Carolina Press, 1976

Farrer, A. 'On Dispensing with Q' in D. E. Nineham (ed.), *Studies in the Gospels. Essays in Memory of R. H. Lightfoot*, Oxford, Blackwell, 1955, pp. 55–86

Fortna, R. T. 'Redaction Criticism, NT' in K. Crim (ed.), *Interpreter's Dictionary of the Bible, Supplementary Volume*, Nashville, Abingdon, 1976, pp. 733–735

Gast, F. 'Synoptic Problem' in R. E. Brown, J. A. Fitzmyer and R. E. Murphy (eds), *The Jerome Biblical Commentary*, London, Chapman, 1968, pp. 1–6

Goulder, M. D. *Midrash and Lection in Matthew*. London, SPCK, 1974

Hayes, J. H. and C. R. Holladay. *Biblical Exegesis. A Beginner's Handbook*. London, SCM, 1982

Henry, P. *New Directions in New Testament Study*. London, SCM, 1980

Neirynck, F. 'Synoptic Problem' in R. E. Brown, J. A. Fitzmyer and R. E. Murphy (eds), *The New Jerome Biblical Commentary*, London, Chapman, 1990, pp. 587–595

Neirynck, F. 'Synoptic Problem' in K. Crim (ed.), *The Interpreter's Dictionary of the Bible, Supplementary Volume*. Nashville, Abingdon, 1976, pp. 845–848

Perrin, N. *What is Redaction Criticism?* Guides to Biblical Scholarship, New Testament Series. London, SPCK, 1970

Sanders, E. P. and M. Davies. *Studying the Synoptic Gospels*. London and Philadelphia, PA, SCM/Trinity Press International, 1989

Smalley, S. S. 'Redaction Criticism' in I. H. Marshall (ed.), *New Testament Interpretation*, Exeter, Paternoster, 1977, pp. 181–195

Stein, R. H. 'The Proper Methodology for Ascertaining a Markan Redaction History', *Novum Testamentum*, 13 (1971), pp. 181–198

Stein, R. H. 'What is Redaktionsgeschichte?', *Journal of Biblical Literature*, 88 (1969), pp. 45–56

Streeter, B. H. *The Four Gospels. A Study of Origins*. London, Macmillan, 1924

Styler, G. M. 'The Priority of Mark' in C. E. D. Moule (ed.), *The Birth of the New Testament*, London, Black, 1981, pp. 285–316 (Excursus IV)

Throckmorton, B. H. (ed.), *Gospel Parallels. A Synopsis of the First Three Gospels*. Nashville, TN and New York, Nelson, 1979

Tuckett, C. M. *Reading the New Testament*. London, SPCK, 1987

Tuckett, C. M. *Q and the History of Early Christianity. Studies on Q*. Edinburgh, T. & T. Clark, 1996

Tuckett, C. M. 'Redaction Criticism' in R. J. Coggins and J. L. Houlden (eds), *A Dictionary of Biblical Interpretation*, London and Philadelphia, PA, SCM/Trinity Press International, 1990, pp. 580–582

Wenham, D. 'Source Criticism' in I. H. Marshall (ed.), *New Testament Interpretation*, Exeter, Paternoster, 1977, pp. 139–152

Williams, C. S. C. 'The Synoptic Problem' in M. Black and H. H. Rowley (eds), *Peake's Commentary on the Bible*, London, Nelson, 1962, pp. 748–755

Chapter 5: Introduction to the Synoptic Gospels

Redaction criticism and the Gospel of Matthew

Barclay, W. *The Gospels and Acts*. London, SCM, 1976

Bornkamm, G., G. Barth and H. J. Held. *Tradition and Interpretation in Matthew*. London, SCM, 1963

Grant, F. C. 'Matthew, Gospel of' in G. A. Buttrick (ed.), *The Interpreter's Dictionary of the Bible*. New York/Nashville, Abingdon, 1962, pp. 302–313

Hill, D. *The Gospel of Matthew*, New Century Bible, London, Oliphants, 1972

Kilpatrick, G. D. *The Origins of the Gospel according to St. Matthew*. Oxford, Clarendon, 1946

Kingsbury, J. D. *Matthew, Structure, Christology, Kingdom*. London, SPCK, 1975

Luz, U. *The Theology of the Gospel of Matthew*, New Testament Theology, Cambridge, Cambridge University Press, 1995

McKenzie, J. L. 'The Gospel according to Matthew' in R. E. Brown, J. A. Fitzmyer and R. E. Murphy (eds), *The Jerome Biblical Commentary*, London, Chapman, 1968, pp. 62–114

Riches, J. *Matthew*, New Testament Guides 1. Sheffield, Sheffield Academic Press, 1996

Rohde, J. *Rediscovering the Teaching of the Evangelists*. London and Philadelphia, SCM/Westminster, 1968

Stanton, G. R. (ed.) *The Interpretation of Matthew*, Issues in Religion and Theology. London and Philadelphia, PA, SPCK/Fortress, 1983

Stendahl, K. 'Matthew' in M. Black and H. H. Rowley (eds), *Peake's Commentary on the Bible*, London, Nelson, 1962, pp. 769–798

Viviano, B. T. 'The Gospel according to Matthew' in R. E. Brown, J. A. Fitzmyer and R. E. Murphy (eds), *The New Jerome Biblical Commentary*, London, Chapman, 1990, pp. 630–674

Redaction criticism and the Gospel of Luke

Barclay, W. *The Gospels and Acts*. London, SCM, 1976

Barrett, C. K. *Luke the Historian in Recent Study*. London, Epworth, 1961

Caird, G. B. *The Gospel of St Luke*, The Pelican Gospel Commentaries. London, Penguin, 1963

Conzelmann, H. *The Theology of St Luke*. London, Faber, 1960

Drury, J. 'Luke, Gospel of' in R. J. Coggins and J. L. Houlden (eds), *A Dictionary of Biblical Interpretation*. London and Philadelphia, PA, SCM/Trinity Press International, 1990, pp. 410–414

Fitzmyer, J. A. *The Gospel According to Luke*, Anchor Bible, 28, 2 vols. New York, Doubleday, 1986

Flender, H. *St Luke. Theologian of Redemptive History*. London, SPCK, 1967

Franklin, E. *Christ the Lord. A Study in the Purpose and Theology of Luke-Acts*. London, SPCK, 1975

Green, J. B. *The Theology of the Gospel of Luke*, New Testament Theology. Cambridge, Cambridge University Press, 1995

Karris, R. J. 'The Gospel According to Luke' in R. E. Brown, J. A. Fitzmyer and R. E. Murphy (eds), *The New Jerome Biblical Commentary*, London, Chapman, 1990, pp. 675–721

Keck, L. E. and J. L. Martyn (eds), *Studies in Luke-Acts*. London, SPCK, 1968

Lampe, G. W. H. 'Luke' in M. Black and H. H. Rowley (eds), *Peake's Commentary on the Bible*. London, Nelson, 1962, pp. 820–843

Maddox, R. *The Purpose of Luke-Acts*, Studies of the New Testament and its World. Edinburgh, T. & T. Clark, 1982

Marshall, I. H. *Luke. Historian and Theologian*. Exeter, Paternoster, 1988

Robinson, W. C. J. 'Luke, Gospel of' in K. Crim (ed.), *Interpreter's Dictionary of the Bible, Supplementary Volume*, Nashville, Abingdon, 1976, pp. 558–560

Rohde, J. *Rediscovering the Teaching of the Evangelists*. London and Philadelphia, SCM/Westminster, 1968

Sloan, R. B. *The Favorable Year of the Lord. A Study of Jubilary Theology in the Gospel of Luke*. Austin, TX, Schola, 1977

Stuhlmueller, C. 'The Gospel According To Luke' in R. E. Brown, J. A. Fitzmyer and R. E. Murphy (eds), *The Jerome Biblical Commentary*, London, Chapman, 1968, pp. 115–164

Taylor, V. 'Luke, Gospel of' in G. A. Buttrick (ed.), *The Interpreter's Dictionary of the Bible*, New York/Nashville, Abingdon, 1962, pp. 180–188

Tuckett, C. M. *Luke*, New Testament Guides 3. Sheffield, Sheffield Academic Press, 1996

Redaction criticism and the Gospel of Mark

Anderson, H. *The Gospel of Mark*, New Century Bible Commentary. Grand Rapids, Eerdmans, 1981

Barclay, W. *The Gospels and Acts*. London, SCM, 1976

Best, E. *Mark. The Gospel as Story*, Studies of the New Testament and its World. Edinburgh, T. & T. Clark, 1983

Best, E. *Disciples and Discipleship. Studies in the Gospel according to Mark*. Edinburgh, T. & T. Clark, 1986

Drury, J. 'Mark' in R. Alter and F. Kermode (eds), *The Literary Guide to the Bible*. Cambridge, MA, Harvard University Press, 1987, pp. 407–417

Hengel, M. *Studies in the Gospel of Mark*. Philadelphia, PA, Fortress, 1985

Hooker, M. D. *The Gospel according to St. Mark*, Black's New Testament Commentaries. London, Black, 1991

Hurtado, L. W. *Mark*, New International Bible Commentary, 2. Peabody, MA, Hendrickson, 1989

Kee, H. C., *Community of the New Age. Studies in Mark's Gospel*. Philadelphia, PA, Westminster, 1977

Malty, E. J. 'The Gospel according to Mark' in R. E. Brown, J. A. Fitzmyer and R. E. Murphy (eds), *The Jerome Biblical Commentary*. London, Chapman, 1968, pp. 21–61

Martin, R. P. *Mark – Evangelist and Theologian*. Exeter, Paternoster, 1979

Marxsen, W. *Mark the Evangelist. Studies on the Redaction History of the Gospel*. Nashville, New York and London, Abingdon/ SPCK, 1969

Nineham, D. E. *The Gospel of St. Mark*, Pelican Commentary. London and New York, Black, 1968

Räisänen, H. *The 'Messianic Secret' in Mark*, Studies of the New Testament and Its World. Edinburgh, T. & T. Clark, 1995

Rohde, J. *Rediscovering the Teaching of the Evangelists*. London and Philadelphia, SCM/Westminster, 1968

Schreiber, J. 'Die Christologie des Markusevangeliums. Beobachtungen zur Theologie und Komposition des zweiten Evangeliums' in E. Grässer (ed.), *Die Markuspassion. Eine Redaktionsgeschichtliche Untersuchen*, Berlin and New York, De Gruyter, 1993, pp. 362–391

Schulz, S. 'Mark's Significance for the Theology of Early Christianity' in W. R. Telford (ed.), *The Interpretation of Mark*, Edinburgh, T. & T. Clark, 2000, pp. 197–206

Schweizer, E. *The Good News according to Mark*. London, SPCK, 1971

Telford, W. R. 'Mark, Gospel of' in R. J. Coggins and J. L. Houlden (eds), *A Dictionary of Biblical Interpretation*, London and Philadelphia, PA, SCM/Trinity Press International, 1990, pp. 424–428

Telford, W. R. (ed.), *The Interpretation of Mark*, Studies in New Testament Interpretation. Edinburgh, T. & T. Clark, 2000

Telford, W. R. *Mark*, New Testament Guides 2. Sheffield, Sheffield Academic Press, 1995

Telford, W. R. *The Theology of the Gospel of Mark*, New Testament Theology. Cambridge, Cambridge University Press, 1999

Trocmé, E. *The Formation of the Gospel according to Mark*. London, SPCK, 1975

Tuckett, C. M. *The Messianic Secret*, Issues in Religion and Theology, 1. London and Philadelphia, PA, SPCK/Fortress, 1983

Tyson, J. B. 'The Blindness of the Disciples in Mark', *Journal of Biblical Literature*, 80 (1961), pp. 261–268 van Iersel, B. M. F. *Mark. A Reader-Response Commentary*, Journal for the Study of the New Testament Supplement Series, 164. Sheffield, Sheffield Academic Press, 1998

Weeden, T. J. 'The Heresy that Necessitated Mark's Gospel' in W. R. Telford (ed.), *The Interpretation of Mark*, Edinburgh, T. & T. Clark, 2000, pp. 89–104

Wilson, R. M. 'Mark' in M. Black and H. H. Rowley (eds), *Peake's Commentary on the Bible*, London, Nelson, 1962, pp. 799–819

Wrede, W. *The Messianic Secret*, The Library of Theological Translations. Cambridge and London, Clarke, 1971

Index of authors

Index of passages

Index of subjects